# HUGE
# DREAMS

----------------------

ALSO BY MICHAEL MCCLURE

# MICHAEL McCLURE

# Huge Dreams

## San Francisco and Beat Poems

PENGUIN POETS

PENGUIN BOOKS
Published by the Penguin Group
Penguin Putnam Inc., 375 Hudson Street, New York, New York 10014, U.S.A.
Penguin Books Ltd, 27 Wrights Lane, London W8 5TZ, England
Penguin Books Australia Ltd, Ringwood, Victoria, Australia
Penguin Books Canada Ltd, 10 Alcorn Avenue, Toronto, Ontario, Canada M4V 3B2
Penguin Books (N.Z.) Ltd, 182–190 Wairau Road, Auckland 10, New Zealand

Penguin Books Ltd, Registered Offices:
Harmondsworth, Middlesex, England

First published in Penguin Books 1999

3   5   7   9   10   8   6   4   2

LIBRARY OF CONGRESS CATALOGING-IN-PUBLICATION DATA
McClure, Michael.
Huge dreams : San Francisco and Beat poems / Michael McClure.
p.   cm.
ISBN 0 14 05.8917 1
1. San Francisco (Calif.)—Poetry.   2. Beat generation—Poetry.
I. Title.
PS3563.A262H84      1999
811'.54—dc21          98–47393

Printed in the United States of America
Set in New Caledonia

# ABOUT THE COVER PHOTO

"The Last Gathering," North Beach, City Lights Bookstore, San Francisco, 1965. Photo by Larry Keenan.

Lawrence Ferlinghetti holds the umbrella above the head of Michael McClure, who is looking up and past Allen Ginsberg; a seated Peter Orlovsky points out of the picture. Others are Stella Levy standing next to umbrella, David Meltzer wearing scarf, Daniel Langton in horn-rims, unidentified dark-haired young man, Richard Brautigan in white hat, actor Gary Goodrow in fez, Nemi Frost in Ray-bans, painter Robert La Vigne seated, Shig Murao (co-owner City Lights), Larry Fagin (poet and editor), Beat poet Lew Welch, and fur-hatted Leland Meyerzove slipping out of the picture at bottom.

# CONTENTS

# INTRODUCTION
## "In Dreams Begin Responsibilities . . ."

"A new world is only a new mind," the poet W. C. Williams had insisted, "and the mind and the poem are all apiece." The endless frames, visions, *realities*, wherewith we contrive to see the place and time in which we live, become in a real sense those very lives we presume as our own. Again as Williams insisted, "Only the imagination is real." So Shakespeare's advice may be read: "We are such stuff as dreams are made on . . ."

*Huge Dreams* . . . It is as if the years in which these poems came to be written had to be salvaged, rescued from an exhaustion and despair that still threatens us, still persuades the vulnerable to grasp for privilege, power, an isolating bastion of whatever kind. The film *Dr. Strangelove's* manically paranoid characters may now be thought simply funny. But they were no joke at the time, rather an ironic word to the wise that whatever responsible control one had thought to be the case had long since disappeared. Terrified kids from god knows where sat with fingers alert to press the fated button as and when the countdown arrived at zero. Home owners were advised that they could secure a government bulletin at the local post office, telling them how to build a bomb shelter in the backyard. Escape routes and righteousness were the common preoccupations.

Small wonder that one had to fight to regain the authority of feeling, to be able to recognize, as these poems vividly insist, the pain, the brokenness, the uselessness of living only in static habits of depression, inert, emptied patterns, in shattered minds. No doubt each generation must invent itself to survive. Each life does so "come into" itself, finds its way in the common world. Michael McClure provides a crucial text defining our crisis in *Scratching the Beat Surface*, where he is able to trace the agencies of human circumstance and need with great clarity. Given the exceptional range of his resources, one thinks of Goethe and of a time when poets were not at some paralyzing distance from the full complement of human thought and perception. What idiocy would so divide thinking, putting one aspect of its possibility in this box, another in that? The Nobel laureate Francis Crick said of McClure's work: "The worlds in which I myself live, the private world of personal reactions, the biological world, the world of the atom and the molecule, the stars and the galaxies, are all there; and in between, above and below, stands man, the howling mammal, contrived out of 'meat' by chance and necessity. If I were a poet I would write like Michael McClure—if only I had his talent."

Hard to believe I first met Michael over forty years ago. The freshness and intensity characteristic of his work here still maintains a physical edge, a sense of active presence. As with D. H. Lawrence, or with William Blake, Coleridge, or Shelley, the body is unremittingly particular in all that he writes, and the voice of each poem is a living one. He was immensely attractive as a young man, and has still the aura of a reflective, enduring beauty. It is not easy, as he makes clear. He works so determinedly to recognize and admit his physical body into what must be otherwise only abstract echoes.

He was living in a communal household in San Francisco with his wife and daughter, together with friends as Jim Harmon and Ronald Bladen, a sensible company of young artists attempting to discover ways and means in the resistant world of that moment. It was, however, one which included a brilliant gathering of others equally confronted, Allen Ginsberg, Edward Dorn, Gregory Corso, Jack Spicer, Robert Duncan, Gary Snyder, Jack Kerouac, Phillip Whalen, who spent much time in the McClures' subsequent household—many, many others, both men and women. He had come from Kansas and tells a lovely story of going to New York for the first time with his boyhood friend, the artist and filmmaker Bruce Conner. They were both just finishing high school and Michael felt that Bruce should meet the great artists of his respect. So they went to various galleries, only to find them closed for the summer. All shut down! But on characteristic impulse Michael found a phone book and located numbers for some of his friend's heroes, and called. Thankfully one answers and listens to Michael's story of their odyssey to New York. Michael tells the great man that his friend is also to be a great artist and that it is fitting they have chance to meet and to talk. So, miraculously, they are invited to come to the artist's studio and the imagined conversation actually occurs.

No doubt such apparent luck is finally the reality of art, that it knows beyond the rational merely, anticipates and intuits both need and possibility. Much else might be said in the way of usual explanations, but a call from two such vulnerably young persons, on a very hot day in New

York, who want, as one says, just to talk, rarely meets with such response. The story sticks in the mind because of the emotional poverty of that time, still broken from the effects of a major war and seemingly flooded with voracious powermongers. An unspeakable righteousness pervaded the usual mind, permitting some as Senator Joseph McCarthy to exercise an absolutely vicious, legalized process of public slander and for others as the Rosenbergs to be executed with a smugness that still terrifies. Another war with a grotesquely paranoid "leader" was also in full swing, as one says. "The Lonely Crowd" and "The Man in the Gray Flannel Suit" were one and the same person.

In such times of communal displacement, when "poverty is the only thing that money can't buy," it matters immensely that some coherent imagination of a possible world be secured. Whatever its pathos, and however vulnerable the attempts to realize it, there must be a "world elsewhere" when the one given has turned on the very people who are its constitution. It is not a time simply for anger or resentment. Franz Kline said (or Frank O'Hara said for him), "Bohemians are people who can live where animals would die." That takes thinking, like they say. Just so, the America of McClure's coming-of-age is one adamantly resistant to the very dreams he hopes to share with others. But it has at least the perverse virtue of "calling the people together," alerting each person—as he so vividly and persistently has proven himself to be so awake—to stand up, to trust despite risk the common bond. Almost fifty years later it echoes as a resonance of immense feeling, that others might be admitted, that others might be found, that there *were* others, truly.

So these poems are the rituals, the gestural and locating language, the invocations of a communal soul or mind. Of necessity they range far from the enclosures of what Charles Olson called an "epicene poetry," a verse determined by the patrons who define it, permitted by secured taste and habit. Reading them, one feels the edges of usual place begin to melt, almost shimmer, as they disappear and the reader comes into a space of much larger nature, and much older than any apparent time. "Before our histories began," McClure's friend and elder, Robert Duncan, writes. "From a well deeper than time . . ."

As his fellow poet for all the years of work this book now begins, I've been delighted and transformed by his writing continually. He's taken me in mind to such unexpected places, whether in poems as are to be found here in this great, initiating collection, or in his extraordinary plays, which are so playful yet always with a reality that reconvenes one's own musing wonder and questioning. *The Beard,* a masterpiece, would take a lifetime to respond to in its dispositions of *person,* of what we have made to live in, the determined embodiment of our habituated world. His novels, *The Mad Cub* and *The Adept,* are both rite-of-passage narratives, which locate the reader uniquely in the transformations of adolescence, in the first, and in the second, the chemical production of invisibility, cocaine. It was Michael who first wrote of the effects of a drug in a literal way ("Peyote Poem"), neither approving nor condemning, simply (complexly!) transcribing his own knowledge. And then there are works such as his "autobiography" of the Hell's Angel Freewheelin Frank. His friendships with people so usefully far from "literature" as a social fact are instances of his own way of valuing life—the actor and artist Dennis Hopper, the scientist Sterling Bunnell, the tragic but brilliant musician and composer Jim Morrison, who was also a poet of real order.

Perhaps poetry was not supposed either to enter or to care about a world which was not to be found in the approved books. Thus it is that Michael McClure shares a place with the great William Blake, with the visionary Shelley, with the passionate D. H. Lawrence, with his old friends Allen Ginsberg, Charles Olson, and Robert Duncan. It was McClure who called Bob Dylan "The Poet's Poet," in a lead article of that title in *Rolling Stone.* It was his song Janis Joplin sang, making them both a little better off: "Oh Lord, won't you buy me a Mercedes Benz? My friends all drive Porsches. I must make amends . . ." Ecology is where one lives.

But we're at the beginning, not the end, and where we are going, there will never be one. Believe me—*sweet dreams!*

Robert Creeley
Waldoboro, Maine
July 30, 1998

# The New Book/ A Book of Torture

*—AND COLD TIRED EMPTY TO BE SO SPREAD IN AIR*
*is Hell too.*
*The predator's world is space. Time the instant*
*taken in the strike.*
*But to be spread to strike at so many unwanted*
*half-desires. Is Hell too. To be so*
*self-flung in so many ways. To leap*

*at so many half-loves. To fall back*
*and find that part of you*
*still hangs there so many times.*

*HELL PAIN BEWILDERED EMPTINESS.*
*The part left smolders.*
*Does not burn clear and drifts too*
*upon the air. Hot Hell*
*is freedom.*

# ODE TO JACKSON POLLOCK

Hand swinging the loops of paint—splashes—drips—
Chic lavender, *duende* black, blue and red!

Jackson Pollock my sorrow is selfish. I won't meet
you here. I see your crossings of paint!
We are all lost in the cloud of our gestures—

—the smoke we make with our arms. I cry
to my beloved too. We are lost
in lovelessness. Our sorrows
before us. Copy them in air! We
make their postures with our stance.

They grow before us.
The lean black she-wolves on altars of color.
We search our remembrance for memories
of heroic anguish. We put down
our pain as singing testimony.
Gouges, corruptions, wrinkles, held loose

in the net of our feelings and hues—
we crash into their machinery making it
as we believe. I say

we. I—You. You saw the brightness
of pain. Ambition. We give in to the lie
of beauty in the step of creating.
Make lies to live in. I mean you. Held
yourself in animal suffering.
You made your history. Of Pain.

Making it real for beauty, for ambition
and power. Invented totems from teacups
and cigarettes. Put it all down

in disbelief—waiting—forcing.
Each gesture painting.—Caught on
to the method of making each motion
your speech, your love, your rack

and found yourself. Heroic—huge—burning
with your feelings. Like making money

makes the body move. Calls you to action
swirling the paint and studying the feeling

caught up in the struggle and leading it.
For the beauty of animal action
and freedom of full reward.
To see it down—and praise—and admiration
to lead, to feel yourself above all others.

NO MATTER WHAT—IT'S THERE! NO ONE

can remove it. Done in full power.
Liberty and Jackson Pollock the creator.
The mind is given credit.

You strangled
the lean wolf beloved to yourself—
*Guardians of the Secret*
—and found yourself the secret
spread in clouds of color

burning yourself and falling like rain

transmuted into grace and glory, free
of innocence

containing all, pressing experience
through yourself onto the canvas.
Pollock I know you are there! Pollock
do you hear me? !! Spoke to himself
beloved. As I speak to myself
to Pollock into the air. And fall short

of the body of the beloved hovering
always before him. Her face
not a fact, memory or experience
but there in the air
destroying confidence.
The enormous figure of her mystery

always there in trappings of reason.

Worked at his sureness. Demanding
Her place beside him. Called

from the whirls of paint, asked for
a face and shoulders to stand naked
before him to make a star.

He pulling the torn parts of her body
together
to make a perfect figure—1951.
Assembled the lovely shape of chaos.
Seeing it bare and hideous, new
to the old eye. Stark
black and white. The perfect figure
lying in it peering from it.
And he gave her what limbs and lovely face
he could
from the squares, angles, loops, splashes, broken shapes
he saw of all with bare eye and body.

# FOR JACK KEROUAC / THE CHAMBER

IN LIGHT ROOM IN DARK HELL IN UMBER AND CHROME,
I sit feeling the swell of the cloud made about by movement

of arm leg and tongue. In reflections of gold
light. Tints and flashes of gold and amber spearing
and glinting. Blur glass . . . blue Glass,

black telephone. Matchflame of violet and flesh
seen in the clear bright light. It is not night

and night too. In Hell, there are stars outside.

And long sounds of cars. Brown shadows on walls
in the light
of the room. I sit or stand

wanting the huge reality of touch and love.
In the turned room. Remember the longago dream

of stuffed animals ( owl, fox ) in a dark shop. Wanting
only the purity of clean colors and new shapes
and feelings.
I WOULD CRY FOR THEM USELESSLY

I have ten years left to worship youth
Billy the Kid, Rimbaud, Jean Harlow
IN DARK HELL IN LIGHT ROOM IN UMBER AND CHROME
I feel the swell of
smoke the drain and flow of motion of exhaustion, the long sounds of
cars the brown shadows
on the wall. I sit or stand. Caught in the net of glints from corner
table to dull plane
from knob to floor, angles of flat light, daggers of beams. Staring at
love's face.
The telephone in cataleptic light. Matchflames of blue and red seen
in the clear grain.

7

I see myself—ourselves—in Hell without radiance. Reflections that
we are.

The long cars make sounds and brown shadows over the wall.

I am real as you are real whom I speak to.
I raise my head, see over the edge of my nose. Look up

and see that nothing is changed. There is no flash
to my eyes. No change to the room.

*Vita Nuova*—No! The dead, dead, world.
The strain of desire is only a heroic gesture.
An agony to be so in pain without release

when love is a word or kiss.

# DEEP CLOUD

We're in the middle of a deep cloud.
Plong plong Plong. The vibes
play to the end. Miles weaves in and out.

Can you see my face, Beloved? Where
are you. I'm here. Oh see
me in the mist of love. Beloved.
Remember that we are close. Hold
me beloved. Put your hands, voice,
through the cloud. Hear
the sweet short song rising upward.

# ODE ON THE END OF JAZZ

We smoke, I watch my eyes by candlelight in the mirror

the cigarette an emblem of ourselves.
I love my eyes, my brows, your hands.
The warm yellow light—

TO WRITE AN ODE I WRITE MYSELF—AM I ALONE?
With Bud Powell's music in the room. With memories of Parker
and thoughts of men that made it. It is this easy that
I write the words pulling and extending into the past.
THESE TYPING HANDS ARE MY OWN

with urge to make it like those men.

TO WRITE AN ODE I WRITE MYSELF—AM I ALONE?
We smoke, I watch my eyes by candlelight in the mirror

the cigarette an emblem of ourselves.
I love my eyes, my brows, your hands
the warm yellow light
that flickers as it glows.

We burn, I burn myself for love. Like madmen swinging
in the dark. With no light
but ourselves. With dreams of self and death
of art.

# FOR CHARLES OLSON

( from depression / a shape of Spirit and occasion )


THIS IS THE ROOM OF THE SERVICE OF FORMLESS LOVE
FOR IT HAS NO FORM!
HAIR IS FUR AND NAILS ARE CLAWS AND EYES SEE OUT!
WE ARE HEROES LYING ON OUR GOLDEN BEDS!

PERSEPHONE! OSIRIS! BEAST! BLACK SERAPHIM!
ROSY FACES PEERING FROM AN UNLIGHTED CAVERN
—WE ARE!
Breathing moves us. BREATH IS. . .
This is my hand with 5 fingers. This is my formless
love and hate.
I despise what death is.
And politics and all of tainted things.
No blood is faintly spilled
that changes. This is love to say it. I know
love who've never felt it.
Inventing it anew.
Making triumph causes the jaw
to clench. There's no triumph
but failure. No love, no love, no love,

already cast. America
is dying—falls down about us.
Break, break
thru till cells are eyes. Kick

in the walls of seeing and of feeling!

---

We are love, love whatever animal we see in
the other. This is chaos, truth
and change. / Elegies
are dead.


And love a cheating thing who dreams cast from him.

# A FANTASY AND COURTLY POEM

OH DREAM OH LOVE OH DREAM OH RACK OH PAIN—
                    EDGES OF VIOLET PINK NEON
slip into the room. Past coal blue windows. Into the room
we move. I love myself. Is this our watch by white curtains? Ferns
spray into the air over us, unfold from pots as signs of time.
Are these my features facing you? Your face is pale
and strained. Is this our dream our last simplicity? No breath
comes from us, or laugh. Love or rack or pain or. We
breathe but what do we ask for? Is this a chase? Are we
figures in a tapestry?

Am I your huntsman as you set a trap for me?

*July '58*

# ODE FOR SOFT VOICE

And sometimes in the cool night I see you are an animal
LIKE NO OTHER AND HAVE AS STRANGE A SCENT AS ANY
AND MY BREATH AND
energy go out to you.
And see love as an invention and play it extemporaneously.

And I who cannot love can love you.
OH THIS THIS THIS IS THE HURT / THAT WE DO NOT
KICK
down the walls and do not see them.
And I do not ache until I scent you. And I
do not scent you. Breathing moves us. Breath is . . .

And more than this that we are huge and clear
and open—locked inside
and moving out and we make outlines in the air the shapes
they are. And we shift so. We move and never keep our forms but
stare
at them address them as if they were there. This is my hand with
5 fingers, my heart nerves lungs
are there and part of me
and I move.
I have no form but lies and drop them from me.

I am a shape and meet you
at our skins' edge.
We change and speak and make our histories. I am all I feel
and what you see and what you touch.
There are no walls but ones we make.
I AM SICK CONFUSED AND DROP IT FROM ME
The nerves are dead that feel no hunger or pain there's no triumph
but failure. This is the last speech of seraphim or beast sick in need
for change and chaos. The room of banished love for beauty. The
tooth in our breast. What we see is real and able to our hand, what
we feel is beauty ( BEAUTY ) what we strike is hatred, what we scent

is odorous. This about me is my bride if I kick aside the forms of it for woman world and mineral for air for earth for fire and water for table chair and blood.

# FRAGMENT OF A HYMN

OH
memory


Fenris chained to himself. Prometheus the Epicurean
of agony.

# LINES FROM A PEYOTE DEPRESSION

((THERE IS NO TIME OF LOVE IN PAIN OF LOVE OR
FACES IN THE AIR SEE

I call them and they do not come. But still
they're there as I am high I shift my eyes about within
the room and see the space. India-prints. Green fantastic-
patterned curtains on one wall. Gold-umber velvet drapes

with light light white and unseen. Showing the space.
Between each thing. Marking there is no time but space.
And you stand within it all. Are there. Are all. No

but part of. Are real. As I see red and green diamonds
( like kachina markings )
on the wall. Positive as I see them to be above the curtain.
( Abstractions of the face of food and water )

As I move my eyes past the purple velvet sofa. Scratched
brown floor. Orange-pink
rubbings. And this is no start to what I have to say and is
not real.
THAT ALL IS COLD COLD AND EMPTY EMPTY COLD
COLD AND THAT IS ALL

-------------------------------------------------------------

I mean simply there is no space and we are solid
figures here within it. But more than this. There are eyes
( this is the lie
or not )
and sights of love. Space is cold and empty.
Or has no temperature and is filled with what is real. ))

AND THIS IS A LOSS AND MEANS NOTHING

except that I am down.
A sad repeat.

To start poorly is no loss to anything.
THAT ALL IS BLUE-GRAY ( OR CLEARER ) EMPTY AND
COLD

and I can't go on.
! Or go on—that this is not a mood! But the way
that matter is—and love.
AND I DON'T KNOW WHAT TO SAY FROM HERE
There are stars far away and cold    to eyes so hot
we measure them. In space and cold
COLD COLD COLD COLD COLD COLD
COLD COLD COLD AND FAR AWAY
and we are not cold in our space and not cool
and not indifferent. And I do
not mean this as a metaphor or fact.
Even the strained act it is.

Bending by the brook and filling cups.

# THE ROOM

AND THIS TOO IS THE ROOM OF HATED HOT SORROW
                                              AND BOILING JOY
Mercy, Pity, Peace and Love enact themselves
in mockery. Are gifts of hand and eye. Empty
of themselves. The unending riff. We are disgraced
by honesty
to see our love stand alone, alone.
This is the agony in the offered hand, the tear
in the turned down eye.

# THE STRAIN

*How hard the bee strives to become a horse.*
—LORCA

*Wer weiss, ob der Geist des Menschen aufwärts fahre,*
*aufwärts fahre, aufwärts fahre, und der Odem des Viehes*
*unterwärts unter die Erde, unterwärts unter die Erde fahre?*
—*ECCLESIASTES* / BRAHMS

THE STRAIN I AM PUSHED INTO THE STRAIN IN
DAYLIGHT I DO NOT CARE I CANNOT
concentrate
BLACK BLACK BLACK AND GOLD AND THE COLOR OF
BLOOD.
I am nerves and bone and hearing. Taste touch and smell.
I pick up the photograph and this is me:

Year-and-a-half old, posed for a portrait—the boy—
sees out past the photographer, unwise eyes, frightened,
round head, animal ears.
On a black bench, the body slumps tense
to the set pelvis, the bare legs, big,
stretch, rest, in the air.
White high shoes. The right hand
hangs to the bench—the left bends to rest,
hand on the hip.

Dark collar with a round neck, angora collar
edge, cuffs turned back to a white stripe,
a gray snake-man woven into the belly,
lines of white dots. His hands
are strong. The thumbs jut. He is sure,
and curious and frightened.
He looks. Ready! Plump mouth slack,
eyebrows high, the senses fine and ready.
The nose small and open—
air rises upward to the platen of smelling,
the eyes shift to receive all in the swing
of seeing,

**19**

body relaxed, hand ready to grasp, feet to run.
Watching.
There are blurred trees, clouds, a river, on the wall hanging
behind.


And I remember the scratch of wool and sodden mornings
and who I am.
And what has happened since,
Mother!

# YES TABLE

YES AND HANDS AND ARMS YES TABLE DARK SQUATTY
AND STRONG
at night I lie in pain and sorrow,
in shadow I am a seraphim—miserable and sick

my dreams are not memories,
so much is blotted out that I am only here.
So much to remember, so much to remember, so much to
remember.
This is a war. The instant's
history.
( In the night I awoke and remembered you and you were gone

though you lay by my side. I searched for you among the silver

hangings, I could not speak your name. I wandered in the long hall. )
etc.

# FOR ARTAUD

1.
The nets are real—heroin ( sniffed ) clears them. Peyote

( 5 buttons )
dispels them forever perhaps. Or until we come out
and smear ourselves upon all we see or touch. It is real!!

They are real! We are black interiors. Are battlegrounds
of what is petty and heroic. Projecting
out all that is base and slack from us. But
not far enough!
And not all—but part / of all / a minute quantity to foul
the air.

And not base and petty but the struggle ( heroic )
and its opposite. As we writhe to see
they cohere and cannot
see it.
OH BEAUTY BEAUTY BEAUTY BEAUTY BEAUTY
BEAUTY IS HIDEOUS
We are black within and sealed from light.
And cannot know it. To move

out from / there / where it is black and mysterious
thru desire and reaching.
AND NOT TO PROJECT THE BASE AND SLACK!

2.

( OH HERAKLES OH UNKNOWING MAN I WILL BE LIKE
YOU AND ACT
and not know myself.
Not to question love or hate and to suffer
for my mistakes.
No webs about my seeing no doubt about my feeling.

Let my hand be as strong as the soul ( the interior )
I know is there.
I am free and open from the blackness
I am so strong I can say there is loveliness and not be touched
by it.
Let me feel great pain and strength of suffering.
My eyes are clear and my voice shakes from joy.
I am strong in my crying. Strong in my blackness
for a lady I love.
Strong for my child in the world.
Let me see out from my seal into the colors and shapes.

Let me know the blackness to see from. What is real
occurs within and moves out. )

3.

YES YES THIS IS THE TABLE THIS IS THE CHAIR THIS IS
THE AIR
I breathe.
But I am not here. I know I am within  and all outward
are acts.
I move from my skin grasping out in desire.
OR MY WILL MOVES ME TO THIS

and I fail,
there are webs about my feeling and clouds about my touch.
And I am out upon all I see and nothing
can return me.
THERE IS NOTHING TO KNOW. I KNOW ALL FROM MY
BLACKNESS
All that I see is real all that I touch.
I am here within and know it.
My skin is the cliff of my being and I
have fallen from it.

Love will not help and not simply truth.
This is the edge ( of my being ) and I peer from it.
I have returned to the souls
STOMACH AND BRAIN.

/ AND ALL ALL ALL

4.

The face is love—the head is clouded by the smoke we make
of it. Shows madness.
Swirling burning and vacant. A superhuman
devotion to make it tell its lies. Do not
LIE TO ME IT MAKES ME SUFFER TOO TO SEE
your face.
I CANNOT STAND THE PAIN WE MAKE BETWEEN US
and I cannot sleep at night.
And I cannot stand the touch of your projections

on my cheeks and arms. The real nets
that lie within the fact of seeing. The sick

signs we cast on all things. Don't throw
them in my face I am weak
and they gather about me / too / . The genitals
are purity and make
the shapes ( like hands ) of love.

The nerves are weak or strong and pass from interior
to exterior and join
us at our edges.

## 5.

MY BRAIN MY BRAIN MY BRAIN THAT I STUMBLE WHEN I
WALK

I do not see the table. My stomach when I talk

that all I feel is hatred
for myself. And I am proud. Without pride. I stand
leaned on myself. I hear myself mumble.
When ( I know ) I am black inside and sealed from light.
And I spread    in the open air
am myself's protagonist.
There's no pain from it but sickness smoke
and vacancy.
Where is my error? In my cells? Protein, acid chains?

What is my sickness and my vacancy? / I care
for love and will not
serve it. And it will not move to serve me.
In my chest ( dull ache ) and knee
( twitching ).
And I do not act from spirit or
from individuality
from my black and inner animal and being.

6.
This is the ache ( remembered ) of my present being
    that I do not desire and move from it
BUT ACT AND SWINGING LOATHE MYSELF FOR
                                   INSINCERITY

          and throw poisons
    ( that do not matter ) in the air and breathe
        them in again. And
      hate myself for acting and for
          breathing.
I WILL NOT BE SICK BUT BLACK STRONG AND REACH
                                   FROM IT
    I don't have love but what is turned from within.
      There's no love for me to ask for. But what
    is turned out to me. I am sick and weak from sick-
      ness and I hate it. Here is love turned
          from me.
    Poison thrown outward to make a radiance
      and not a net or web.
These are two lines drawn from me and pulled
      to me from    myself.

7. _____

    That we are animals—this is my paw—my eyes see out!
    I love you from deep inside from my very edge.
THE TRUTH IS VIRTUAL. LOVE LOVE APPROXIMATES TO
                                    MAKE
             its manner known.
      Bone teeth nail and cheeks ankle ( and ) vein.
    I cannot ( can ) swing to you thru body and pain.
          Is nothing! A song.
       I am not virtual and speak alone.
    Is a song lost in lack of feeling and comes from the edge.
     I am sealed in light and spread to my
  outer skin. Where only blindness keeps my cells
        from being eyes.
STOMACH BRAIN AND BODY ARE THE ROOMS OF OUR
                                   LIVES
         and they are filled with blackness
         for we need no light
     except about us. If skin is eyes and fingers
        and there is no virtual speech
          or acts or
          love.

## 8.
## AND ALL HUGE AND ALL /


I am a flask sealed and nothing is happening!
I am black and I do not move out. See
nothing. Or for an instant I am tall look down
on all as it is fit
for seeing. That all is water clear and running,
solid and wavering,
that all is real and I walk in it. Among it.

And see in a face or breast an animal
loveliness.
And feel my chest and stomach beat for it.
AND IT IS NOT LOVELINESS! BUT CLARITY BUT PURE
responding. When I see
a breast I love. Or face of suffering.
In the cold water black worms ( planarians )
move and dart or crawl unseen.
And all is clear holy and not beautiful
to them.
But icy light icy dark and green wet leaves
above.

# RANT BLOCK
*for Jay DeFeo*


THERE IS NO FORM BUT SHAPE! NO LOGIC BUT
SEQUENCE!
SHAPE the cloak and being of love, desire, hatred,
hunger. BULK or BODY OF WHAT WE ARE AND STRIVE
FOR. ((OR
there is a series of synaptic
stars. Lines of them. It's that simple
or brutal. And, worst, they
become blurred.


SNOUT EYES
As negative as beauty is.))
LEVIATHAN WE SWOOP DOWN AND COVER
what is ours. Desires
OR BLOCK THEM. SICKNESS—ACHES.
Are heroes in simplicity with open eyes
and hungers. Truth
does not hurt us. Is more difficult than
beauty is. We smolder smoke pours
from our ears in stopping what we feel.
( free air )
Your hand, by your side, is never love.


FORM IS AN EVASION! POETRY
A PATTERN TO BE FILLED BY FAGGOTS.


WILD ANGER MORE THAN CULTIVATED LOVE! !
Wolf and salmon shapes free to kill
for food love and hatred.
Life twists its head *from side to side* to test
the elements and seek
for breath and meat to feed on.
I AM A FIRE AND I MOVE IN AN INFERNO
sick I smolder
and do not burn clear.

Smoldering makes nets of smoke upon the world.
I am clean free and radiant and beauty follows this.
Not first but follows.
What is love or hatred but a voice I hear
of what I see and touch. Who is the man
within that moves me that I never see
but hear and speak to? Who are you
to stop me? Why are you here
to block me? All I choose to see
is beauty. Nerves. Inferno!
Fakery of emotions. Desire for presumption. Love of glory. Pride.
Vanity. Dead and unfilled desires. Regrets. Tired arms. Tables. Lies.
BLOOD AND MUSCLE BLOOD AND MUSCLE BLOOD
AND MUSCLE BLOOD AND MUSCLE
Calling pure love lust to block myself and die with that upon my
head?
Wit and false stupidity with no point to it but the most tangled ends
unwitnessed by myself in fulfillment. When I found you sleeping
why didn't I? Would you love me for it? Do I care? OH. And smoke.
AND NOT THAT FINE SWING
of wing or fin!

And never chivalry. The strive to rise. The act of grace. Of self.
Of sureness large enough for generosity. The overflowing.
But the chiding carping voice and action. What is this? Why
DON'T WE KICK IN THE WALLS? KICK IN THE WALLS!
INVENT OURSELVES IN IMAGES OF WHAT WE FEEL.

WHERE HAVE ALL THESE CLOUDS OF SMOKE COME
FROM?
I am the animal seraph that I know I am!

And I burn with fine pure love and fire, electricity and oxygen
a thing of protein and desire, !!
and all of this is ugliness and talk not freedom
OH SHIT HELL FUCK THAT WE ARE BLOCKED
in striving by what we hate
surrounding us. And do not break it in our strike
at it. The part of us
so trained to live in filth and never stir.
THAT I WAIT FOR YOU TO RAISE YOUR HAND FIRST

( to me )
This is sickness. This is what
I hate within
myself. This
is the war I battle in. This is the neverending instant.
The black hour that never ceases. This is the darkness about
the burning.
The form and talk of form as if flames obeyed without
dwindling.


These are the dull words from an animal of real flesh. Why?
Where is the fire in them?
Never let them stop until they are
moving things. Until
they stir the fire!
Never let them stand stemmed by form again. Let
my face be radiant and give off light!
Never allow sign of love where hatred dwells!

If there are bastions, let my love be walls!

# THE COLUMN

I AM BEAST O BEAUTEOUS MUSIC GLORIFICATION
                    PRIDE MOVEMENT MOTION
Beasts' Hearth
((( this is )))

the sparkling firelight flashes on us
I AM

pride!

And what falls torn, disjointed, liberty what
! TORCH !
Spirit, warm vapor, rises solid, a wavering column
from the butchered
mouse, Haydn, Mozart, whale, shark, tossed
arm, leg, torn from the soft, the belly,
gut the steaming streaming, viscera
sent forth. The Whole. Unclashed. Heard

within. The monster of pure Love. Vision,
the cold thing of warmth,
uncompromised blackness
radiating colored light. I am what I see

the flame reflected from all things
THE BRIGHT COALS OF ALL RAISING SCENT

HEART AND COILED, THE TRACERY GLEAM
of pink meat
unfurrowed from blackness.
Laid fallen on the table sending half-spirals of flames
making light within to the outward object.
The torn and bloody fur black and dripping. The heavy stench rising
from it clogging the nostrils. The gouts on the fingertips.
The black and pearl and translucent opal.
What passes through the Ghosts of Loves. What does not leave trails

on the air. What burns in blackness. What does not sleep
or dream.


Single, discrete, a fanged mouth, thin beast-mouthed
NO! A NIGHTMARE!
Twist out of sight out of shape into a distorted monster
of gleaming eyes, taut limbs, veined and sinuous
the whore of the sick mind.
The tail-tip!
THE RISING SPIRIT FROM THE WARM TORN LIMBS,
THE LOVE
of body torn from the body. No, floating
above it hangs. Is beneficent. Emotionless, free of the
lover, the beloved, stretched below.


IS AS I SEE IF FIRST IS THE COLUMN OF BEAUTY FROM
THE RENT SHAPE
BEAUTY IS WARMTH THE FLASH WE MAKE UPON ALL
THINGS
in one case.
And I who stand apart am not aloof.
Discrete but not disparate from pain
I see
or sights rising warm from the corpse
I see.
Am spotted outwardly ( with marks ) but inwardly draw close.
Respond and twist so. Cry with
what I see.
Even cry with joy at sight of it.
Spirit is measurable is the exact shape of our bodies.
And at moments expands and dissipates
never to return to anywhere but hangs
THE BEASTS' HEARTH
DEATH SEX GODHOOD ARE ONE ARE ONE
process. When
we rise to it. Oh white face oh agony oh splendor
OH STREAMS OF LIGHT


pour from me—I tear off the mask
and find the face ( of agony ) my face

beneath the mask. My face,
my features there beneath,
stemmed
from the corpse. Beneath
rise up the flame tips the head
is balanced on.
Blood!   Blood!
The blackness there within sweeps out and kindles.
OH CHRIST OH DEATH OH HELL PERSEPHONE!!!!!
flames and flowers of the torn-out-moment.
And stand calm / excited and bloody-beaked in the rising column
of spirit. Blinking at the
raised force.
Feel the blackness in me raise in heat and sympathy

IN LOVE.
And stand stalwart before it.

# L'ÉTOILE, THE STAR

*from the tarot*

ON THE GOLD HEATH THE NAKED WOMAN BENDS
SHOULDERS FORWARD,
knee to the ground, earth, foot to the earth

she holds red cups or chalices and pours herself.
Her hair is blue, lined in waves as the stream
beside her. Over her head are eight great stars as she
is a star. Red, yellow and blue. With seven

points and one with sixteen. As she is a star in the desert.
A compass.
As she guides the spikey black bird in the tree behind her
when it is night. The bird is
impatient, nervous, waiting for night in the bright
desert.
The tree waits for the coolness of night to breathe.
The stars are there in the heat. Seen
in the day by those who know. The bird. And woman.
Who is a star. With round breasts. And red chalices.

A CARD: her face is sad and yearning and she is not touched
by heat. There is a dandelion
and artichoke behind her and they are of her past
she does not have or need. Aloof
sad yearning busy and cool in the desert born
of heat and she is a figure.
Her toe placed at the water's edge almost beneath the pouring
of the cup as if she were bathing
herself with herself. From the other
cup water flows about her foot and (?) into
the stream. She has no need

and is a star.
And is as untouched by water as a star.

It is day and there are dunes. There are stars and they are unseen
by all but those who know. They
are there real as night. Figures
repeat themselves.
Are gone and static as the past. As a mulberry tree
growing from the sand. Or a bird
feeding on it.
A CARD: Her face is sad and yearning and she is not touched
by heat. There is a dandelion
and artichoke behind her and they are of her past
she does not have or need. Aloof
sad yearning busy and cool in the desert born
of heat and she is a figure.
A CARD: she is a woman coming from it.

# THE FLOWERS OF POLITICS, ONE

THIS IS THE HUGE DREAM OF US THAT WE ARE
HEROES THAT THERE IS COURAGE
in our blood! That we are live!
That we do not perpetrate the lie of vision
forced upon ourselves
by ourselves. That we have made the nets of vision real!
AND SNARED THEM

OH I AM BLIND AS A FLOWER AND SENSE LESS
we see nothing but banality.
Break in the forms and take real postures!

This is the real world clear and open.
The flower moves and motion is its sense,
and transference of ions,
all that it does is perception
and vision.
OH BREAK UP THE FORMS AND FEEL NEW THINGS
I declare that I am love who have never known
it and I make new love.
My hand is pink and white and blue and great
to me. My eyes are bright
and I know that love is air. An act
and nothing more. That we are seraphs,
cherubim and heroes, chieftains and gods.
This is the blind senseless thing of knowing
that unconscious we walk in it, and strive
among all things. This is
A CANDLE
and shape of light.
The hand and arm annunciate all things

and draw the eye upon the speaking face

declaring from the inner body.

We are wrought on a bending shaft of air and light
and make an animal around it

and spread a radiance from ourselves that melts
in light.

# THE FLOWERS OF POLITICS, TWO

ONLY WHAT IS HEROIC AND COURAGEOUS MOVES OUR
BLOOD
we are lost within ourselves and tangles
of a narrow room and world if we do not speak out, reach out
and strive from individuality. This is
WHAT I HEAR IN HEART NERVES LUNGS, NOT ELEGIES.
I am a black beast and clear man in one. With no
split or division. But from one without.
AND WALK IN IT FREE
as flowers or blood
and hate the forms of it you make
destroying it to take it from my touch
and sight. I hate
you in the night when I am whole and free.
And I know you will be stamped out by your forms
and invisible revolutions and I

do what I will and can to speed them on.
THOSE LEFT WILL BE GODS AND SERAPHIM
and need no memory of you—
only this is more than beauty
without holiness and self-conceit.

Your sickness poisons you and you
are dying. No aid
or speed can save you. And I
am free!

Free of politics. Liberty and pride to guide you. You pass
from ancestral myths to myth of self. And make
the giant bright stroke like that madman Van Gogh.

# A SMALL SECRET BOOK

**1. For Philip Lamantia**

YES GOD THE DESIRE HANGS THERE UNFILLED TURNS
INTO SMOKE!!
I TURN AND FLY BEFORE IT, AFRAID OF THE HIDDEN.

What will I do, fill my mouth with sweetness? Turn down
the love? Whip myself with fear? Afraid
of the scared.
Twist in the midst of a seventeenth century
pink *concetto?* The pink heart
flies into ( making ) a cloud, the eye
heaves and backs in fear, trembling!
SAY INSTEAD HOW THE SHARK FEELS. OH
I am sick!!
Christ, God, Lamb release
the pressures.

Empty me from woodenness to bitterness!!
FILL THE LAST BLACK HEART.

**2.**

OH CHRIST GOD LOVE CRY OF LOVE STIFLED FURRED
WALL SMOKING BURNING
who am I that I feel pain so? What is the flower
before my eyes that I call it fire. Nasturtium,
why the twist of petals why the writhe of the pale green
stem? Why do I see you and feel lamb. Why are you the
shark that moves out upon me? Why are you flame
that you burn me. What is love
that I fly from the feel of it. Why am I filled
with the soft wool pressure? Oh what is pain
THAT IT ALL FLOWS
that I move in my aching sleep?
that I censor, censor, censor. BLESS ME.
Pour me into the soft arms that I am
ever stiff.

3.

THE SHARK IS THE LAMB. THE KILLER WHALE THE
LOVER.

WHAT IS THE OH FORM OH, OH SHAPE OF BLACK
LOVE. WHAT IS MY HEART
that I run from it? What is love that I pull
myself to meat to hide from it. Where is the fear
of pride leading me?? Oh what are your breasts on
my arm? That
I weaken beneath them? Oh why are you so light
and I so heavy?
Why do I make myself a phantom before your anxious stare?

What is the dream I have of you? Why do I lock my cock
and heart from you? What is Heart? Why do I hold
the movement down. Why do I twist and turn so? I
move out to you. Why do I want you so
that I am sickened? So much I want you. What
do I hold within that tears
me. Why do I lean in weakness against the blade
of myself? Why are your breasts so light
on my arm.
5/25/59

4.

OH CHRIST OH GOD OH FUCKING SHIT OH SHIT SHAPED
PAIN OF LOVE!
Oh unpulsing pressure outward against my ribs
and stomach against the soft muscle and bone
showing how weak I am that I lose myself before
it relenting and weak, speechless. Only
eyes pleading to the smoke rolling out of my
mouth. I stare from my blue cloud.
EYES STARING FROM MY BLUE CLOUD
Do you see me in sadness and love?!
Traitor to my mean grasp for you! Fake
to what is black and felt. Stifling

the urge to love you to death. To kiss
you and eat your soft skin.
To roll in juicy Eros. To
turn to roiling merry flesh!

BLESS ME
FOR WHAT I FEEL IS WEAKNESS AND IT SWELLS
in me turning to weakness
becoming huge. Love devouring
love and swelling unfelt huge and pours
or seeps out finally. I who am
blessed am unblessed. Oh. Oh. Oh.
LOVELY WOMAN.


## 5. For Thelonious Monk

ALL IS COOL AND BOUNDLESS AS A ROLLING LAMB OF
JAZZ, I SEE
the shades slipt behind me. Avalokiteshvara!
I am blessed and protected. I hear the beauty
of the tossing notes. I am safe!
It does not matter Love, Avalokiteshvara, Kwannon,
love you pale beauty;
see my twisted head and face grow
thin again.
PURSUE THE SLIM SHADES IN AND OUT LOST IN IT ALL
hide you from myself., choke
on my love for you, happy
for an instant.

( All is fire and I fat myself to be a candle. )

( Careful, careful crazy man and burning heart. )

OH! OH! OH! OH! Tired old fear. OH! OH!

# A COOL
# PAMPHLET
-------------------------

# ODE TO THE ROSE

THE ROSE IS THE POINT IS OPEN WHITE-PINK PETALS
                              SPREAD INTO THE AIR
        to my heart to my eye. The stamens and pollen.
        The stem thorns. The wood-green leaves, the twist
            and search for light. The rose's face.
        The open petals. The ugliness of the instant. The beauty
        of the final act in the move of change.
                        •

THE HARD SOFT SCENTED SHAPED AND BREATHING
                    SWEET ODOROUS
GODDAMNED AND SINGING SILENT SOFT AIR AND
            cold shapelessness made perfect in this
            blessing HAH! cold thing I move
        before or sit in rapture unable to stare

I LOVE YOU LOVE BREATH DO NOT TOUCH ME COLD
                                        THING

                UNDREAMING
            Am I here? Am I here?
        Tough line of wood surmounted by the pink-white
                not face not fair.
                        •
        Breathing and unbreathing light solitary
ROSE BLANK ROSE UNCOUNTERED UNDREAMING
                              UNDREAMING
            HEAVEN!!


PHANTOM I, NEAR YOU MOVE REAL MEAT, FLESH ARMS,
                                    CLOTH SHIRT.
        Move in my wooden Hell. That is not Hell or Paradise.
            The other thing the Truly Hell. And see
            you are another thing. Hold Heaven folded. Shit
            Hold Heaven. Make sweetness there about.
        NOT SWEETNESS BUT WHAT YOU ARE

in coldness. What you are. Show what you
raise from wooden stem. Make pain for me
of what you are.
That I am cold cold without footing.
I DO NOT LOVE OR HATE YOU BUT LOVEHATE YOU
am a phantom before the pink-white swirl the open
face of what you are the airy thing of solid
matter. The dying action that you are before my
eyes
the poor cut flower risen from the earth,
stem, bitter, nitrate sweetness, water,
sunlight. Passed from leaf
to brightness. Risen from the black
fact. Isolate as the crap I write upon this page.
I AM PHANTOM HERE BEFORE THE THING OF MATTER
am unreal before the sculptured rose

THE WHITE-PINK MATTER
the face before me staring at me, eyeless.

NOT FACE, NO
but petalled thing. Sweeping
there before me. The eye cannot see enough.
OR ROSE ROSE LEAF PETAL BLACK IN ITSELF OF LIGHT
OF MATTER
solid what is the wrenched how is the    is thing I cannot
look at it. Within my eye
now late within the sight within the chain
of vision sight real here thing gone existent
cold formed thing warmed by the sun. Without
anything except the existent sight of what
I see. The rose. The . . .

I wake thinking of you and pass
THE DAY WITH YOU WITHIN MY EYES
CANNOT LEAVE YOU THERE
behind and
DO NOT FILL MY EYES WITH SIGHT OF YOU.

---

Here now the rose is real does not move
in any way in time or space is filled with.

ROSE LEAF PETAL BLOSSOM PISTIL LEAF THORN SPINE
edge stem pollen scent is moving still inodorous.
Out of the sight of this failure
THIS
evening. Held.
Or I mean holding, is, its, Heaven.
Petals opened Heaven. Thing there
CLEAR SO CLEAR. SOMEWHERE LIKE THE CATERPILLAR
wrapped wrapped. The babe's face staring out.
Or the children's books. The things lost, the Leaf
Children's march to the gates of Spring. Oh,
Love, Oh, the old song. Do
You hear? The shock to see and speak so.
That finally so much is true. That we are left
with nothing. Empty. And.


OH CHRIST OH GOD OH SHIT OH!! GNAW!! GNAW!!


AND NOTHING


but the long long pause. The moment. The rose
THERE BEHIND MY HEAD. THE THING
of it.
ROSE! ROSE! ROSE! ROSE!
White-pink from the red-brown
stem. The wood-green leaves. The rising
OF THE WHOLE THING FROM THIS BLANKNESS I
DESPISE
and I too. Rose. Rose. The white-pink
thing of all. From the less than limbo, the bare air
Emptiness of no light all shitting goddam thing empty
house hate bare shitting oh stopped thing of cold
MATTER ROSE MATTER ROSE MATTER ROSE
( Trick stop begin. I forgive. )

1. OR AM I AND WHAT IS OH  THE SIGHT OF ALL ABOUT
TEARS
into flesh and bone into the dry word always removed
from the pure sight. Or rather the pure sight
is here and unescapable. The pure sight is bare and cold.
THE LOVE THE DREAM
the attachment is what we love. I love
the pure sight. But what is left. Oh
WHAT IS LEFT? WILL
you give me all of it. Here it is a gift.
Take the pure gleam gladly. Remember

the bareness.
REMEMBER, THE ROSE, FIST, TENTACLE OR WHAT YOU
SAW.

2. GATHER THE SIGHT CALL OUT. I CAN'T. IT WILL NOT
COME OR BRING
to me fresh love. I am locked with inert memories.
I drip them behind one by one. The sense of emptiness
replacing the sense. The thing of nothingness
becomes larger. The sense of emptiness fills
a space with itself. The animal. The brown eyed
moving sense of action, grace swings dispersing itself
does not show in hallucinations in dreams in aspirations
passes before my eye not. But makes itself known
without glamor. Glamor ( FOUND IN THE EYE OF THE
WATCHER ),
as I fulfill become what I watch no longer watcher.
I fill out becoming what I desired to be. Empty.
Only the cry of pain is fulfillment.
What I feel and fear to say. To scream.
To allow new beginning. To Allow
breath without glamor.
FLOWERS ACCRUE.

To truly allow the shape of it feared!

# OH GRACE OR OH LOVELY SWING BRIGHT COLORS!!


FLOWER RED, NASTURTIUM ORANGE, PAIN ORANGE
FLAME RED
Hot carbon particles. Red hot the fire

that is. The smoke.
Again the smoke again. The shoot of the hot
burning part into its . . . Cry. Oh Why . . . Where?
So.
NEVER. NEVER.
Remember only the cry. Cry.
The Ultimate. All else
is relative. The rose itself a cry. As I.
Who can hear the animal cry. As we see the flower.
A confusion. As truth comes out into

the Oh Well. Stop, again, repeat.
As we writhe to move in grace. As the words
say . . .


THE ANIMAL SOFT FURRED WITH HUGE BROWN EYES,
The SERAPH who is man's
face with snake body. ( Where
is that snake headed man? In
Egypt? )
FURRED ANIMAL, SERAPH FLOWER, NASTURTIUM-ROSE.
I am all of these and none of them.
The voice of myself here.
AND NOT NOT NOT RELATIVE. NOT
just sick of this.


THE CRY IS A ROSE!!
all things begin with platitudes,
ow!
The skin is broken!

THE SCALES GLEAM PURE LIGHT RADIANT OF THE FACE.
The worm with the babe's face. As explain-
ation. I, solid before the memory the image,
WRITHE IN MY BURROW
in my flesh. Or imagine so, that I
do.
And struggle with the fantasy I do not have
or recognize. I hear perhaps the cry.
Perhaps see the light. Wondering

of this pure instant where are then my
aspirations. Oh short line. Oh tossed and boring
burrowing. In this cartoon. Oh peace. Peace. All fear more
than I. Do I face it? Strike
out for what I know and see. Slit my throat
over my bowl. White bowl. The red
dripping. OH. OHHHHHHHHHHHH. No wit not even
Shit fakery shit. OhhhhhhHHHHH.

*HOMAGE TO WOLFROBE*
MEMENTO MORI
SKULL

I fasten my eyes on the rose. The rose
is a skull. A confusion.
CONFUSION

HOMAGE TO WOLFROBE
who sees himself as a sack of skin
he fills by his will
and empties against his will
who looks out darkly on the moving plain
through dark eyes and a sunken face
emptied and seamed by age
like a bag.
WITH FEATHERS IN HIS HAIR.
Brown cheeks creased and dry.

THE ROSE THERE COLD COLD AND FRAGRANT A MILD
scent. I see within my eye in the chain
the rose. The rose nothing. I am removed

from the sight.
Can I see the rose without sight
of myself?

Can I hear the cry? Can I be real? Can I ignore
the rose? Oh solitary shit kill
burnt bloody ohohohohohoho mine corners.
Can I aspire to the pure form. Can I face
the pure arms? Will my face be rapt of joy
without the opposite? Oh Freedom! Oh Shakiness!
I CANNOT FACE THE PERFECT.
Inspiration exists and it's the last word that
what we pretended to believe is true.
It is a pain and shakes me. At last
that there is no escaping the truth of the lie
we live by.

I FORGIVE I FORGIVE I FORGIVE I FORGIVE.

# FOR JANE

((OH CHRIST OH GOD OH SATAN BEAST SHIT ANIMAL
to see the animal beauty in the rose.
The eye's petals. To Hell with confusions. Hell is confusions
I see the swing of the animal grace in the
stillness of the rose. Captured
the slithery grace of the snake. Caught the
goddamned forgotten thing in the stillness
of the open face of the rose. How can we,
how can I fight perfection? How can I help
but see? How can I want to fight that cold
perfection lies indifferent to itself, how
can I deny my confusion? How can I deny
that I quest myself. How do I chase what
is about me past catching. It is here.
Neon and pink. Unseen on the air it demands
a wall to fall on. As the paw or tentacle that thing
to scratch upon. Upon upon. The murdered
beauty scratching the herb of itself.
Division is neither here nor without.

The wall itself is not indifferent. In
different the wall is not indifferent. The Plaster
waits for the slow motion, the move of the pink
light upon itself it is still in gloomy darkness.
The floors are black not without color. All
is cool waiting upon the thing that comes
constantly out of itself. As a snake say
as much as a rose is a snake. As much as my
body moves within itself. As I twist in
shame upon what I say and do not feel. Do you
see the rose? The cry is lunacy is indifferent
not to the hearer. Is not indifferent. Demands
that someone listen. Would not do this without
listener. At moments I have this backward.
Tho it is real as a blue pool or a color.
I do not forgive in forgiving. Ultimately. It is the

cry and the paw moving, tentacle, over the wall
or petal. Never never stopping.

What I force to stir and what moves without
motion. Wolfrobe. How I do not see lightning.
Who says. It is cool in the night before the long
white curtain. The brass is cool on my arms
as a blossom. The pink
face is open to me within and I open to it
that which sees. I am never there without it.
I cannot draw it to me and it won't come.
Oh sing. Sing. The noise the sound goes on forever.
I love and regain contact. There are new red
bright roses. They rise to the wall climbing
like hearts and hands. Like the sentiment
of beauty without the fright. Like gentle
mice light red-purple. Themselves no answer.
Oh now. Now. Begin again shitting house hate
bare. The herb of murder. Contained within

the space of room. Like
Ghosts. Banshees. Fear Ghorta. Waterhorses.
The dreams of childhood. The snake.
The alligator under the bed. Looking
for pink toes.
Escape escape forgiven shakiness!!

Appear real rose cold and unburning!! ))

# BLUE ROSE

This is the harsh turned bitter biting sad blackened
blue rose. Blue Rose of love. Soft as an arm.
Oh give me
your arm. Let me out of this
pink room. I forgive you,
again. .
I want Hallucinations and Animal Color!

To hear pain and cry out!

THE GODDAMED BITTER FUCKED COOL AND SWEET
DARKNESS OH
this is my room! This is my sweet gray stillness.
That I dream within. This is my head lighting the dark
these are the spots of light that glint from my
scales.

# POLLEN

THIS IS THE OH AH CALM STILL COOL GRAYNESS SELF
HATE
pollen. I
re-unite with myself. In sadness in misery,
feel my gray hands all that is left of me
but eyes. Eyes to see the minute variations
the multiplicities of color.
Blue grays, gray grays, pink grays, violet.
All that sags in a cool room.
All all vacant as eyes! Vacant
as soft furs and love.
FUCK SHIT CUNT HUNG
on myself!
The room the room is a soft jacket.
Love. The room is a rose. With pink walls
I dream and pity myself within!

# LA PLUS BLANCHE

JEAN HARLOW, YOU ARE IN BEAUTY ON DARK EARTH
WITH WHITE FEET! MICHAEL
slaying the dragon is not more wonderful than you. To air
you give magical sleekness. We shall carry you into Space
on our shoulders. You triumph over all with warm legs and a
smile of wistful anxiety that's cover for the honesty
spoken by your grace! Inner energy presses out to you in
warmness—

You return love. Love returned for admiration! Strangeness
is returned by you for desire. How. Where
but in the depth of Jean Harlow is such strangeness
made into grace? How many women are more beautiful
in shape and apparition! How few can / have /

draw such love to them? For you are the whole creature of love!

Your muscles are love muscles!

Your nerves—Love nerves!

And your upturned
comic eyes!
Sleep dreams of you.

# Star

*This book is a blast of my poor brain splattered over Hell and Earth & Heaven*

# 13 MAD
# SONNETS

# MAD SONNET 1

THE PLUMES OF LOVE ARE BLACK! THE PLUMES OF
LOVE ARE BLACK!
AND DELICATE! OH!
and shine like moron-eyed plumes of a peacock
with violetshine and yellow on shadowy black.
They SPRAY from the body of the Beloved.
Vanes shaking in air.

---

AND I DO NOT WANT BLACK PLUMES OR AGONY . . . AND
I DO
NOT SURRENDER. And I ask for noble combat
to give pure Love
as best I can
with opened heart.
Love,
I have not seen you before and you're
more beautiful than a plume!

Stately, striding in Space and warm . . . ( Your
human breasts! )
LET ME MAKE YOUR SMILE AND HEARTSHAPED FACE
IMMORTAL

---

YOUR GREY EYES ARE WHAT I FINALLY COME TO WITH
MY BROWN!
AND YOUR HIGH CHEEKS, and your hair rough
for a woman's—like a lamb. And the walking virtue
that you are!

# MAD SONNET 2

OH HOW I WANT THEE FAME!
FAME, THOU VIOLET LAOCOÖN OF TOILING BRAWN
and writhing snakes enwreathed on upturned
GRIEVED FACES.
Oil and sweat shake from the locks of the famous,
and though they moan they are stoic as a tree.
Fame loops out fat coils like a half-forgotten dream
and binds men's wrists in their romantic agony.

---

Fame, you are a rotten plum!
I wipe you from my fingers
with a rosy napkin.

---

LET ME SEE THE LOVE TENDRILS
of woman and child!
AWAY FAME!

My spirit is not trapped by love of fame.

I am not hungry for death's attitudes.

BLESS NIGHT.

# MAD SONNET 3

TINY MAMMALS WALK ON WHITE BETWEEN THE
$\qquad$ YELLOW
BOULDER GRAINS OF THE LILY'S POLLEN.

With minute (milky pinktipped) tits they suckle jet-eyed cubs.
And they make their life labor in clouds of scent
and drink the dewdrop and the rain in caves of hollyhock.
I am obsessed with the thought
THAT I AM SANE
and they are there hearing the sugar run in the stalk
AND THEY STARE FROM MINUSCULE FACES.

I am obsessed with the thought
THAT I AM SANE
and men are not

IF BEAUTY IS NOT MEAT THEN WHAT IS ALIVE
is not imagination!
AND IF MEAT IS NOT BEAUTY
then save condemnation
and drop your bombs
&
spray
the rays!

PEEK OUT! PEEK OUT!

# MAD SONNET 4

Also I am obsessed with knowledge that . . .

I AM OBSESSED WITH KNOWLEDGE THAT . . .

Inspiration may be a dark vapor of blue or black . . .

- - - - - - - - - - - - - - - - - - - - - - - - - - - - - - - - - - - - - - - - - - - - - - - - - - - - - - - -

I have ruined 9 poems attempting
to translate this simplicity
to a shape and an image!!

INSPIRATION may be a dark cloud-jet of blue or black
that arches from the foreheads of men of genius
LIKE SPOUTSPRAY FROM A WHALE OR DOLPHIN.
It rises with the force of shoulders from the spot
between cockbase and anus;
it worships world and woman—
wanting assurance to join with them together for a blissful instant
UNMEASURABLE BY TIME.
Up! Up rises the Serpent Power—a last secret
of the gross physiology
AND BURSTS OUT
to write like squid ink on clear air!

It's real as a fleshy snout
or Alpha and Omega.

# MAD SONNET 5

OH SCIENCE, I LOVE THE TOUCH OF VELVET
and I love the feel of green velvet more than brown.
But mostly I love the burnt spot with the charred edges
where the pink flower print beneath
shows through!
I AM A MYSTIC AND I BELIEVE IT IS TRUE
that my body survives as long as I do.
OH SCIENCE, I am not torch, not light, nor no longer
masochist. And I swear. I SWEAR
that for 300 years Man has grappled with a new consciousness,
and stands on the verge of a Cherubic Civilization
AND
YOU MUST
DESTROY GOVERNMENTS
AND REPRESSIONS
of love-flesh.

------------------------------------------------------------

We must all wear rings of midnight opal
and save hunger for inspiration
AND LOVE TRUTH.

# MAD SONNET 6

AT THE ABYSS OF EXTINCTION each cell
in my heart and physique closing to die
I STOOD AT THE WINDOW
of October night.
I AM A POET NOT A MYSTIC. I wavered to die . . .
But in the black closet of the sky
I saw Titans feasting at a banquet of immortal music
AND I KNEW IF ALL IS PERFECT THERE
ON DEATH'S SIDE, IN THE DARK SUGAR,
in the Negative Universe, in anti-matter, then all is good here
and I turned to cry in loving arms. OH!

---

The Space & Time is a pinprick of nothingness
in a vaster solid universe
dropped through to here by a majestic accident. The Atheist
awaits his swart return on the wingbreaths of Cupid
—and the birth of Self's actions!

---

"YOU CAN EXPECT ME TO BE SINCERE
but not to be
impartial."
—Goethe

# MAD SONNET 7

HEART, BRAIN, AND BLOOD—EACH CELL CLOSING TO
                                                    DIE
with all of the physique's desires set on death.
I stood at the rectangular window of October night
to die by sudden escape of the spirit's electricity.
But in the black chest of the sky
flashed titans at a banquet of immortal music
AND I KNEW IF ALL WAS PERFECT THERE
ON THAT SIDE OF DEATH WITH DARK SUGAR
IN THE NEGATIVE UNIVERSE
that all was good here too . . . and all of the beauties of Anacreon
and Jesus were true. And I turned
to weep in loving arms.
Oh! SAVED BY A REVELATION.

---

WE SHALL NOT BECOME VAPORS OR COAL

---

WE ARE FREE! YOUR TOES
are as lovely as your pearls.
May we each be Satans-of-Love and Gods-of-Love
for an instant
and keep loneliness and beauty
from their death.

# MAD SONNET 8

I HAVE SEEN YOU AGAIN! Your skin is gold brown
flecked with flesh-gold. And your closed eyelids
are pale pink purple with long brown lashes. YOUR FACE
is a network of tiny wrinkles. YOU ARE ALIVE!
YOU CHANGE! YOU CHANGE! YOU CHANGE!

Sleeping, your plumes are down.

Your buttocks are sleek and ageless as Ionian marble.
Your eyes open will be grey or the color of Jade.
THEY CHANGE!

---

We do not change . . . but the walls go down.
As if you were a pomegranate
newly brought into the room
you change the light, the ceiling, air & wood about you.

- - - - - - - - - - - - - - - - - - - - - - - - - - - - - - - - - - - - - - - -

THE SOLID BED BENEATH SHOULD BE A WAVE OR
CLOUD
to satisfy
the genius
of your calves.
YOU GLEAM AS IF RUBBED WITH ANCIENT WAX,
and breathe,

madonna.

# MAD SONNET 9

DO MEN CARE OF WHAT I TRUDGING HOPE TO SPEAK?
I cannot care, there's a surging music in the air—
I hate it and will disrupt it! It's the rhythm and blues
of custom in modern furs. It drives me mad!
I hope to crack the doorways open—MY HANDS AND EYES
are openings to you. Forms and attitude
are mercantile static disguised as melody.
THE BAYING OF THE DOGS OF HOPELESSNESS
harasses
the falcon of the senses
but they grow hoarse.

---

I WOULD RATHER BE AN IDIOT
than blind

---

A FALCON STARES FROM ANOTHER DIMENSION
with his black eyes
and fierce boyish coldness.
I see two cockroaches caress
with gentleness
in the universe and empire created by their love.

FREE!

# MAD SONNET 10

LET ME DRAW FACES ON EVERYTHING THAT BREATHES
OR STANDS,
and give visages to the trillion trillion things that live
and let their spirits out. Give them black bushy brows
like two squirrel tails turned up and out at the edges
and little dots for nose,
and black passionate eyes like scrawled stars
AND LONG, HUGE, SMILING, BOWED, UPTURNED LIPS
to sing concertos
with . . .

OH AMBITION

*FIAT LUX,*
let there be light!
*Ariston metron,*
let there be moderation.

# MAD SONNET 11

I LOVE SEAHORSES, TEDDYBEARS, AFRICAN VIOLETS,
MICROSCOPES
AND AXES but I will not be ashamed!
I am the graceful man of my era.
I LOVE
Killer Whales, and the spiral galaxies,
and Keats, and viruses, and anti-particles,
and the dainty and dark perversity of lovely women
with hooked noses and black hair—or blonde and plump
with slim ankles—Brahms,
MELVILLE, AND MARX (Harpo), REICH, FREUD,
and the juvenile delusions of Einstein.
I like fat and muscle, sweet and bitter,
and all of the Comedy of Glory.

---

AND I SAY,
if the last vast natural philosopher
vanishes—the grizzly bear from the peak—
or the soft hallucinatory moth
from the cactus blossom . . .

- - - - - - - - - - - - - - - - - - - - - - - - - - - - - - - - - - - - - - - - - - - - -

WATCH OUT!
They are not replaceable
by robots

# MAD SONNET 12

DROP AWAY THE MASK of inhuman pretense
to discover if there is Romance!

---

Imagination's brutes disband in harmony
and leave synthetic and chaotic rat-deers of imagined shapeliness.
Pull down that drapery
and give physique to passions, gestures, acts, desires, and loves.

WHAT IS BENEATH THE WEB?
'I am,' I cry, 'and all of my clarity.'
All of the real and unreal conceal and are my being.

THERE ARE NO WEBS!
We may build great spirits and join in the ghostly dissolution.
And those who *can*
swell outward, swirling
like a herculean tantra, swarming in their loves.
The lamblike accrete their humane pleasures
basking in the City garden.
LET ALL POSSIBILITIES BE ROLLED INTO A SINGLE
BALL! *Huh?*

- - - - - - - - - - - - - - - - - - - - - - - - - - - - - - - - - - - - - - - - - - - - - - - - - - - -

Our teeth are mountains to smaller lives.

LET SUPERSTITION DIE—and bad and good be seen
in each man.

# MAD SONNET 13

*for Allen Ginsberg*

ON COLD SATURDAY I WALKED IN THE EMPTY VALLEY
OF WALL STREET.
I dreamed with the hanging concrete eagles
and I spoke with the black-bronze foot of Washington.
I strode in the vibrations
of money-strength
in the narrow, cold, lovely CHASM.

Oh perfect chill slot of space!

WALL STREET, WALL STREET,
MOUNTED WITH DEAD BEASTS AND MEN
and metal placards greened and darkened.
AND A CATHEDRAL AT YOUR HEAD!

I see that the men are alive and born
and inspired
by the moving beauty of their (own) physical figures
who will tear
the vibrations-of-strength from the vibrations-of-money
and drop them like a dollar on the chests
of the Senate!
They step with the pride of a continent.

# FOR AN UNKNOWN MELODY

LOVE AND SEX BE ROSY! ROSY AS A NEW WREATHE
of arms and legs and thighs and tongues and tits
with torsos soft as velvet shields
like sails that float through air
and let the faces there beneath me change
from heart-shaped to another shape
and buttock roll as they trade place.
LET ALL LIPS SMILE!
Look up at me with twinkling eyes!
Now your spirit is newborn.
HAH
AH
YAHH
GROOOOOHR!

# NOVEMBER'S TEXAS SONG

*for Lee Harvey Oswald & John F. Kennedy*


DOUBLE MURDER! VAHROOOOOOOHR!
Varshnohteeembreth nahrooohr PAIN STAR.
CLOUDS ROLL INTO MARIGOLDS
nrah paws blayge bullets eem air.
BANG! BANG! BANG! BANG! BANG!
BANG! BANG! BANG! BANG!
BANG! BANG! BANG! BANG!
BANG! BANG! BANG! BANG! BANG!
BANG! BANG! BANG!

Yahh ooh FLAME held prisoner.

DALLAS!

# SMALL ODE ON THE NEED TO DRINK

*(after Anacreon)*


The Cherubim know most. The Seraphim love most.
I'M A SERAPH
—let me learn
eternally
the shape of the lovely bosom.

—And drink champagne
and write temporal odes
to Drambuie
among the stars.
The black sea drinks and the clouds drink her.
Then why, amongst all creatures,
must not I?

# A ROSE

*(after Anacreon)*

LORD, LORD, LORD, BLUE ROSE!
THE EAGLE HAS ENTERED
my spirit
and I have become divine! Even
to fear death—or pretend that I do—
when now I know, this being,
this reality, THIS DARK THUNDER PINK,
THIS ROAR, this smelling of roses,
this reaching to clutch the petals,
is here.
And needs no duration.
Breathing you.

# THE LION-BEAMS

THE DANCERS . . . THE DANCERS ARE LIONS!
They bow and curtsy
and throw kisses in the air.
Their legs are long and white
and are the legs of humans.
They smile from behind their manes
and whiskers.
They throw kisses in the air,
and turning join their arms
to their partner's.

Nimble paws dancing on notes.

---

All lives are equal—!
Graceful worm elves making
turns that are sweetness . . .
The gyrfalcon swooping
over tundra . . .

---

The universe of anti-matter
proves Nirvana to the atheist.
Lion-beams from the central source
flash on my faces.

# THE PURPLE ONE

The Lion-beams flash to each pinnacle
of Mankind's greatness.
The Central Source rages where time & space
are accident
—and at the outer edge we speak
in radiated genius—
darting love from eye to eye.

The bodies are clean and white
—arm, leg, and thigh rolling on buttock.
The body is a flower!
The tiniest white bloom in the field
staring with minute yellow eye
nestled in fur—is as we are!

The Lion-beams flash among the meaninglessness
making dearness of power and love
almost at random
but guided
by an inner source in the receiver
who casts it on and on and on
giving meaning to the hillside.


AH, but see the purple flower!

# LOVE & STRENGTH

STRONG THINGS ARE NOT OF BEAUTY MADE!
The BLOODY LUNG, the LIMB! The ORGANS draw upon
themselves for reference! Their shapes
are not the shapes
OF BEAUTY
but the gestures traced in air are theirs!
To know what we are, and how we do it
IS FRONTIER.
The dark death of ANTI-MATTER presses
our bulging intuitions. COURAGE IS BEAUTY
—and not strong.

---

I LOVE! I SAY, I LOVE! I love
all beauties and all strengths, and I am wavering
in fear, in weakness, and in love. Perfection's
no accomplishment.
BUT desire is. To feel the self melt
before sheer grace. And sense dissolve in time and space.

---

I am a hunger
left
by strength and beauty,
AND A MAN.

# THE PANSY

SYSTEMS ARE DEATH! THE BLACK AND YELLOW PANSY
HAS NO RULES
but stares with catlike face from clumpy leaves
—a shaggy shapely head upon a tiny stalk.
Look the black is purple!
The jowls droop but the forehead raises high.
A single central eye where petals meet!
The face is flamy splash!
IS THERE ANY LAW BUT LIFE?

---

Need there be a code but that of sigh or cry,
or dream, or silence, or of movement, or of growth?
SWEET AND BITTER JOIN
to lift
a higher thing
that moves in air.
What does *system* mean
to molecules of dry and moist?

---

My mind is lovely as a spruce and I,
and those who love me,
make it mine.

# ODE TO THE NEGATIVE UNIVERSE

*lines written in New York City*


OH MAN, THE TWISTINGS AND ENCLAVES
AND TANGLEMENTS
AND BLANK MISERIES OF PERSONALITY

WILL BE LEFT BEHIND! The tortures
and the agonies will be left off HERE
and cast aside. Assume all of the powers
of idealism and beauty—become rose-mammal
and lily-beast. Feel all
the black mysteries of flesh,
explore the sweetnesses of the Universe
HERE
for this is the highest
to achieve. It cannot drag you.
All will be shed and left behind
AND CAST IN HUGE SOFT FOLDS
LIKE A ROBE. . .


WE SHALL STEP FROM THE BREASTS OF MATTER
TO EXPLORE
into the Negative Universe
where all will be feasting
of the physical spirit with shapes of turmoil
wrested from it.
DEATH IS A BLAST OF THE PHYSIQUE
THROUGH THE MIND.
Assume all real battles and loves. Act here
AND MAKE GESTURES AND ROAR
(but not in the wars of passing illness).
—LET LOVE OR HATE BE NOT REPRESSED.
The smile of conceit is the injury of a child.
I SEE THE GLOWING WHITE FACE
OF BEAUTY
IN THE DARK ROOM! FOR THIS IS A VOID!

THERE IS NOT RAPINE OR FIERCE TERRORS
IN YOUR HEART!
Here all love is matter.
And love matters. And matter must be love.
And there is good and evil.
What matters is the full living. The destruction
of fear of accomplished gesture. For *all* will be dropped
like a robe. Love will not become
armor, hate will not be chain-mail, but all slips
away like a drape of soft fur when the spirit explodes.
THE HUMAN SPIRIT IS THE REAL PHYSICAL
ACTS IT MAKES
and the being passes over to become the intuited
visage of loveliness!
Each day is a terrible battle
and it need not be!
There need not be fear!
All that matters is physique of the human spirit
&
dreamed love's perfection.
IT IS TOO SIMPLE TO SPEAK OF! All the stridings,
battles, agonies, and pleasures ARE the spirit, and they
combine with a latent spirit of the genes
AND THEY CREATE OUR PASSAGE.


I,


WE,


create our passages to the joy and black music of sweetness
that does not await us but that we make
in our acts preceding the spirit's
explosion into liberty. Passivity of men
is poison. In the universe of matter
the spirit of man is unending crisis.


•

OH CLEAR AWAY THE BLOODSTAINED MODELS!
Let fears of hideousness come to an end.
The new era of consciousness
has entered the muscles of man.
THE NEGATIVE UNIVERSE IS THE BLACK
CLOUD OF SWEETNESS!
THE NEGATIVE UNIVERSE IS THE CONSTANT
STATE OF INSPIRATION!
(Inspiration is physical and is the secret hunger
of man for immortality he dare not dream of.)
DREAM AND CONSPIRE OF ALL NEEDS
AND LOVES ASSUMED
to the physical being and then dropped away.
IT IS SO EASY!
THE NEGATIVE UNIVERSE IS THE RICHNESS
FOLLOWING DEATH
without fear.
The Negative Universe is the blackness we explode in.
The Negative Universe is the final achievement
—slipping into the eiderdown of black
with all of the assumed:
LOVES
HATES
BLESSINGS
left behind! But not to be had without the physique-
condition of the spirit. Not without LIVING!!!!!!
PREPARE FOR A WELCOME GLORY
TO DEATH
by real love!
MAN FEEL YOURSELF
and swell like a Herculean tantra. . .

# VALENTINE'S DAY SONNET

GLORIOUS DIVINE CREATURE, I'VE JUST SEEN YOUR
NAKEDNESS,
your womanly-muscled flesh, and lambliness again
in new light.
I SMELL THE SULFUR AND SPRUCE
in your hair. And the dream-scent of your sleek waist.

But it is the relaxed light upon your brow and cheeks
that tells me
YOU MUST BE PROTECTED
from Rippers and Devourers. (They seek
at random gentle beings for torment.
How you must drive them mad!) You smile
simply from reality in back of dreams.
You peer from the soft cliffs into green waves
and make rippling profiles of beauty
everywhere.
WHAT STRANGE THINGS YOU SEE.

I will protect you—for now I know the secret!
Your breasts and lower belly are masters of the science
of higher thought. Your hair and lips belong to a stream
of divinity.
I shall keep your liberation safe!

# SONNET

I AM STILL LEARNING THE SHAPE OF THE LOVELY
BOSOM.
I am a babe and I see my mother's face
upon all other visages. LOVE! I need
love and I am a man with hair upon my chin.
And still I see as at 5 or 14 years the beauteous face!

---

I have pretended many things but the pain is real
as a pearl and as true as I am mammal.
I can not pour out the roaring flood
of imagination and gentle thought unless love flows.
OH MOTHER! MOTHER! LAUGH FOR ME
I shall see your face into eternity.
LET THERE BE A MOVING OF PEACE
between us. My tears are as real as yours.
I am the incarnate of the passing glory
of your loves . . . forever building more for you.

---

OH MOTHER, see me as your loves,
together we are the learners of immortality.
My eyes are stamped with your beauty.
We are a perfection that is ceaseless.
Let there be a warm full calm to FILL the space between us.

# MAD SONNET

WHEN SPIRIT HAS NO EDGE ITS BOUNDS ESCAPE
the Human frame. Men swell to blindness
without pain and are stupefied. Smooth fingertips
receive no pleasure. They become what they call Soul
and are terrified and search out,
in the far flung space they occupy,
their souls again. Never have they left—
but the old ideas are vacant.
Our idea of solid self cannot satisfy.
Surely all boned creatures feel urge
to Spirit-Spread when they desire a thinner Soul.

Even the Kraken and the Daddy Longlegs
have idealist hopes and winters
and move in fright on swift thin feet.

And there are mute mindless creatures
who are themselves the cliffy abysses of their desires
in unending and extensive darkness that we
spread into and fear
as sanity of glory or madness.
Have no fright in our perfection.—Here is the Verge!

# MAD SONNET

WE SHALL BE FREE TO SCATTER
IN THE WORLD OF DESTINY
where Heaven and Hell are a dream
left draped like blue silk upon a useless chair.
But now we have come together by atom, organ, molecule,
and cell. And we must touch and mingle
like bowls of roses side by side
with scents and petals, free, overlapped and intertwined.

The sky is black, white, blue or clear,
or fresh milk curdled with vinegar and burst
and drifted away—and we peer.
But now we are cups of roses and balls of a million
lives to move one arm or fist.
OH, I am the life I am
in sweetest April. Where anxiety is killed
by self-kindness.

We make ourselves in free totality.
We are snake-angel men,
and godly women astir. Hail!
HAIL PRINCE LIFE! HAIL PRINCE DEATH!

# THE CHILD

*for Bruce Conner*


Who were the Lion Men who walked in my dreams
when I was a fat and sleeping babe
in a room whose walls were miracles?
Who were the lion men with faces of fur
and manes
who bent by my crib to bless me?
Was it they who implanted the scroll
that said '*I am the maker of my spirit and soul*'?

---

I see myself as I slept—
all sleeping infants are sizeless and giants
dreaming in a universe immeasurable
with plump legs sprawled upon shining quilted sheets.
AND OVER ME THEY TOWERED
and I was tiny in their passage.
I remember their pointed teeth and whiskers as they stooped
to smile—and the scent of their fur in the room.

------

WHO AM I?—I CAN'T REMEMBER.
But I know
I am the strength
of a million loves!

# UNDER THE BLACK TREES

THE TREES AGAINST THE GREY-PINK SKY ARE NOT
TENDERNESS.

THE COLD DROPS OF RAIN UPON MY NECK ARE NOT
MERCY.

My chest is weeping—and I do not cry longer.
There's only the kneading of my chest
and I know it is moaning. The lobes
of my lungs draw upon one another.
I have made a vow to love—and Love has come
to me and I to love.
I see that vows are not easily made nor broken.
Love has come to me and turned me inside out.
My deep pains are in the world
like the rain and the hovering trees,

AND I
AM WHOLE,
and well, and I have held my vow
through unconsciousness, and I am proud

of the glory of Love that is one thing
and unchanging and ever broadens

to more love.
And I'll smile like an angel
for you, and lie by your side.

# THE SURGE

*for Stan Brakhage*

This is the failure of an attempt to write a beautiful poem. I would like to have it looked at as the mindless coiling of a protein that has not fully achieved life—but one that is, or might be, a step towards living-being.

THE SURGE! THE SURGE! THE SURGE!
IT IS THE SURGE OF LIFE
I SEEK
TO VIEW . . .

Plato and Darwin are the dead heads of glorious vision.

Dante turned to the woman Beatrice
in Paradiso and she spoke:
*"Tis true that oftentimes the shape*
*will fail to harmonize with the design*
*when the material is deaf to answer.*
*Then from its course the creature deviates;*
*For though impelled towards the highest heaven*
*it has the power to bend in other ways—*
*just as when fire is seen to fall from clouds*
*if the first impulse of its natural bent,*
*turned by false pleasure, drives it to the earth.*
*—No more, if I judge rightly,*
*shouldst thou marvel*
*at thy ascent, than at a falling rill*
*that plunges from the mountain to the depths.*
*Twould be as strange, hadst thou stayed down below . . ."*

IS NOT THE OLD MALE BEAST SIGHT OF IT
as dead as Hell?
Our view of Life is still so young and so worn
and ripped by the brutal tatters we made of it!
Subtle Plato and Darwin opened worlds to us by stating

what we knew and our admissions threw us into
reality! How blind is blind?
How deaf and dumb is our dumbness? If we admit,
we do have fresher eyes. There's a calm inertness
of joy that living beings drift to and from. (And it is far
back when the Universe began . . .
and it is here now too.) I do not mean the mystic's view.
Or that of a man locked in the superstition of his own repression.
Not emotive analogies!
I mean there is a more total view!
It shifts and changes and wavers,
and weakens as our nerves do, to finally make
a greater field and more total sight.
We yearn for it . . .

*I love you* is the key.

The Surge of Life may not be seen by male or female
for both are halves. But perhaps the female,
who is unprincipled, sees farther and into more.


2.


OH, HOW I HAVE BEAT MY HEAD AT IT in male stupidity!
And here . . . here in my hand, is a picture of the living Universe
made by a woman as gift of love in a casual moment!
—A valentine in ballpoint ink. The drawing calls all
previous images to abeyance. The dark and radiant
swirlings in my head seem clumsy—tho I trust them too.
It is a tree that is not a tree.
It might be a placenta with thin branches or veins.
The stalk of it narrows to a gasp of life
and stretches downward and spreads into what
might be the earth or the top of another tree.
((Is there a forest?))
(Upon the lower treetop, or earth, lies a creature coiled
and incomplete, with round and staring eyes.)
Intersecting the narrow trunk, or crossing it, in
mysterious geometry, is a palette shape.
Upon it spins around and round, before ascending

up the stalk into the boughs, a creature that
is a ring of meat divided into the individuals
comprising it. They are hot upon each other's
tails. They stare after one another and outwards
with round eyes. Some beasts of the ring
are dots and blobs or teardrops of primal meat.
And some are more whole creatures. Some contain
within themselves, midway, an extra pair of eyes
to show their division is not complete. (Or
to assert the meaninglessness of all division
that is based on eyes or other organs.) Those eyes
deny that a single head or set of senses divide
lifes in a greater sense. *The ring is one!*
The creatures
swell, spring free, and dart up the cincture
to a greater space above.

A long, large, snake-shaped molecule of flesh
coils from the earth
around the palette and caresses the higher branch
in sensuality.
The high part is a heart! Within it a man's head & shoulders
rise from a bat-winged heart with thready tail—
and a heart upon the thread tip. Nearby is a circle
(a vacuole? a nucleus?) with a shape inside that might
be any living thing from a vulture to a child.

High and low outside are stars that are
living sparks or moths.
Turned upside down the drawing means
not more nor less. It is a gentle
tensile surge
a woman views.

3.

Yes, all things flow! And in our male insistency on meaning
we miss the truth. The mountains do pour, moving in millionic
ripples over thousand aeons. Demanding brute reality we forget
the greater flow and then the black immediate is larger—and it is

and isn't. But Life, THE PLASM, does not flow like lead does.
It SURGES! Is that the difference?—And it is one great whole
and isn't. It is something sweeter than we see—we must feel
and hear it too! Male and female have, and do not have, importance.
They matter! *It is not relative but real!*
In black immediate I feel the roaring meat mountain
herds of Bison and of Whales or Men or solid
American clouds of birds 100 years ago.
Then I am moved by meanings and sights of
the smaller surge! Then I, dreaming,
partake in the surge like a Plains Indian
on horseback and I know my smallest gene
particles are forever spread and immortal. Distances
and hallucinations then can cause no fear;
life is primitive and acceptable.

Is all life a vast chromosome stretched in Time?
Simply a pattern for another thing?
But the pattern like the chromosomes *is* the Life,
and the Surge is its vehicle.

It does not matter!

It is the athletic living thing of energy!
All else is *soundless and sightless* pouring.

There is no teleology but
surging freedom.

Inert matters pour in and out of the Surge
and make sound and sight. But neither
they nor the Surge will wait. It is another matter.
Space/Space/Space is a black lily holding the rosy,
full, flowing, and everspreading and con-
tracting, spilling flash.

The woman's easy sight of it can be bolder than the man's
She admits that we can never know, and tells
us that the question is useless words.
The Surge can never see itself for the Surge is
its self-sight. And its sight

and being are simultaneous.
There is no urge to see or feel—for it *is* sight
and feeling.

Except for the glory

GLORY

GLORY

GLORY

GLORY

GLORY

GLORY

it does not matter.


4.


But desire to know and feel are not eased!
To feel the caves of body and the separate
physical tug of each desire is insanity. The key
is love
and yearning. The cold sea beasts
and mindless creatures are the holders of vastest
Philosophy.
We can never touch it.
We are blessed.

Praise to the Surge of life that there is no answer
—and no question!

Genetics and memory

are the same

they are degrees of one

molecular unity.

We are bulks of revolt and systems of love-structuring
in a greater whole
beginning where the atoms come
to move together and make a coiling string . . .

Beyond the barrier
all things are laid upon a solid
and at rest.

Beatrice! Beatrice! *Paradiso is opening.*

WE ARE AT THE GATES OF THE CHERUBIC!

# A THOUGHT

IN MY FANCY I CAME UPON
A SCENE OF CARNAGE . . .
from a snowy cliff I spied
that the heads of Great Men were mountains
looming on the plain.
And ships that were Great Men's faces flew
through space above.
Diving and zooming they blasted
gloomy missiles of their genius
to smash the Mountain Ones below.
The sky was scribbled with fire and smoke.
The Earthbound Ones returned the cannonading.
Peaks cracked with laughter.
THE AIR WAS FULL OF GROANS!
Fir trees on stone ears crackled.
Wings of the Flying Ones wobbled and flapped.
A physicist with sideburns streaming like a cape
was shot down by a biochemist.
His profile crashed screaming into a little lake.
He dragged himself out to be reborn
as a mossy granite bust.
Then he fired from the volcano
of his skull.
The Flyers beat against each other.
The Mountain Heads threw boulders
and stared with bulging eyes
and gnashing jaws.

Heads of Generals moved across the plain
on tanktreads.
Their hats were very straight and the braid was all aglitter.
IS *THIS* MY BRAIN?
I climbed into an eagle's nest
to watch the endless scene.

# THE ANSWER

SEX, HUNGER & INSPIRATION—THE SECRET REAL
PROBLEMS!!!
SOCIAL CONSCIOUSNESS CAN'T extend past human bodies.
Money and Politics are a universe of discourse
entrapping physiques.
Abortion's a little closer. WE MUST HAVE IT.
To stop so much suffering.

AND I WANT TO SEE WOMEN'S NAKED BREASTS!

---

and gracefulness returned to faces.
I have social consciousness
& elaborate dark humor.

SEE

SEE

SEE
-----------
the living

# THE HUMAN FACE

The human face, the human face is a vision
of real flesh, of rose and brown and pink.
—I love the human face!
And the face and brain and hanging body,
for sometimes the body seems to droop beneath the face,
is the Lover of the Universe through its dimmed
fastidious eye. (And sometimes the face
and body knit together into one perfect animal.)
But the human face is a meat jewel
and I love the face
as much
as
hands!
We *are* perfect.

# A THOUGHT

Feel thy depth outpouring on each wall!
Each woman touched is a mammal and each man.
The cool concrete bulkhead is a call
to the senses imagining it
to be a beauty—and a rosy mattress for sleeping on—
where a black-haired girl sleeps
twitching her lion's tail
among the petals.


We are calm tornadoes
swirling in caves of spotted velvet.

# THERE IS NOT PASSION ENOUGH

THERE IS NOT PASSION ENOUGH TO SCREAM OUT!

TO CRY OUT! TO DIE!

AND WE PLEAD FOR LOVE AND BEAUTY TO COME
LIKE FABLED SHAPES
scratching at our windows! To see them
rolling there and writhing for admittance!
We dream for love of god and immortality
—and fear to stretch our arm
for honest joy of what we are.
Yes, we are mammals of blood and vein
and our interiors are cathedrals
of musky smell. It is the hand
put to the breast—and lying side
by side in sexual companionship
that is truly love! Then we
are the clouds of pleasured,
weird and mysterious flesh in strands
of muscles, organs, that stare
and pluck at one another
CREATING LOVE.
The soft vision of a gentle god is crap!
But the creation of each beauty
made between us
is a majesty and awe!

# LOVE LION
## BOOK

---

*For the sword outwears its sheath,*
*And the soul wears out the breast . . .*

—LORD BYRON

OH FUCKING LOVER ROAR WITH JOY—I, LION MAN!

I GROAN, I AM, UPON THE CONE SHAPED BREASTS

& tossing thighs!

—AND SEND MY THOUGHTS INTO A BLACKER UNIVERSE
OF SUGAR!
Thy face is a strained sheer Heart twisted
to fine beauty by thy coming.

It is a million miles from toes to thighs!
(Our bodies beat like the ultimate movie
slowed to blurs of two meat clouds becoming
one—and the Undersoul is joined
by kissing mouths.)


OH!


OH!


And I am some simple cub
with plump muscles, loving immortality!

THE SHEETS ARE WHITE.

THE PILLOW SOFT.

JESUS HOW I HATE THE MIDDLE COURSE!

Thy Eyes! Thy Eyes!

CLOUD, CLOUD, CLOUD WE WRITHE WITHIN
of spirited meat and self-souling flesh.
I am not your mesh
nor you my ultimate—but I believe it!

I believe thy hand is paw of velveteen
of green or black or rose, and thy nail is loving claw
pressed upon my rib!
HAIL THE BRIGHTER TRUTH THAT BURNS MORE PURE!

---

Damn confusions!

---

Hail the black imagined wine we dive
within with bodies wound together!

Praise to your slender arms and sleekness!

Joy to thy slim legs and welcoming BODY!

Eternal honey melling upon thy SPIRIT!

Ten seconds of flesh adorn thy SOUL!

—and that is PLENTY!

This brown and white INFERNO
of pain and joy and work and breath
and agony and pleasure is a mattressed
FLOWER.

## I STRIVE TOO HARD AND DAMN THE GENTLENESS

Peace. Peace.
And silent quiet air that stirs in wave-shapes.
—A universe of wine where ripples
are speaking faces. NO!
THEY CANNOT BE! BUT HEAR
THE HUGE SOULS SINGING AS THEY DRIFT
TO THAT BARRIER BEFORE AN OUTER
PLACE! What lies the body-soul
creates in peace ! ! ! ! !

LIES! LIES! LIES!

BUT FLUIDS dripping in the body make music!
Thoughts dive far into the night
and return with cries
that are similar.
I know they are there
and we
will join them

BUT DOUBT IT!

THE WARMED HAND IS PEACE! !

THE LARGE LAYS THERE

MY HEAD!

YOU.

WHITE BREAD GLEAMS UPON HEAVY TABLES.
No! That's another time long-gone.

Dahlias and ferns are drenched with juice of peaches.
No! That's gone too.

Beat on white walls to let their spirit out!
The royal beauty of the higher thought and energy
project themselves where there is
muscle! The sets
and velvet curtains are reflectors
of the soul's and muscle's self-invention!

GOD DAMN THE SETS! THE FURNITURE and CURTAINS!

And bless and love them!

Bless the bones and skeleton thy body

swings upon. Without them we would dream
in Space—or be nothing!
The smoothness of thy toes,
thy chin
and brassy mane


are parts of love set free
and manifest

THY AMBASSAGE ! !

((OH BLOODY PURITY CONSTRAIN, STOMP OUT THE LIE
AND SWING ! ! ! Deal the death urge with
a higher card. THERE'S NO SUCH THING!

LOVE and BLOOD and SUGAR are the same!
Ideals and Hope are tame
compared to what's within my heart!
Odes are transient breath.))

OH YOU ! !

YOU PERFECT ! ! !

YOU PERFECT PERFECT ! ! ! ! !

You light made flesh in sacred paradise
of room and floor and plaster wall and
steam and vase and oxygen! and book
and pen and ink and glass and cup
and bed and sweeping plant!

Yet where is gentleness?

HERE!

There are no molecules! This moment shall never die!

THIS IS PURE PLUPERFECT ! !

## AND ARE THEY LIES ? ? CAN VISION BE MISTRUTH?

Can I deny it from a damasked world before I feel
the future grief? Red and white. Rose and lily.
Blood and cheek! Thy tanned flesh is good enough
but I am torn and yearn. There's no pain!
This is solid concrete pleasure . . .
Your breast upon my knee and generosity.
The nets you set for bliss
are baited with their key!

OH BLISS-MATE !

Beyond the cloud we make (and in it too)
is vacuum of Soul made up
of spirit-flesh transcended.

Rave on!

Rave!

but listen,
STILL THE SENSES, for an echoing cry of joy!

ALL MUSIC IS SOUL AND SPIRIT-SOUND
OF PEACH-SHAPED FLESH!
Or anything that never dies.
No! I've said that before and gained the key
to Liberty. Let Joy and Liberty and Love
die also. Rise up Virtues!

HEART! CHEST! SHOULDER! MAMMAL-FEELING!
Let there be a mountain where arms
are waterfalls that splash.

I—free of you but coming
to your music!

We—rolling in a cloudy bed
free and clean.

The blackness awaits us as we turn
to spirit.
In ten trillion years
BY CHANCE
and luck
we rise up to kiss again.

Remembering

TRUTH IS LOVE.

AND YES YES YES, THAT'S ALL FOR A NEW BEGINNING!
Prepare the body for an afterthought that lasts
eternally as flesh! NO?? I cannot care.
The intellect passes through the window
& penetrates the mists of another timelessness
that causes mouth to wet and makes spirit
tremble. Hear! Listen! Feel! It's all clear
HERE! We are new beginnings
of a new thing
becoming fresher . . .

We do it now—make whorls of memory,
of meat and nail, upon a thing
that may be changing to last forever

STARS AND NEBULAE—THE SAME MATERIAL.

And faces changing under me from blonde
to dark. You set the nets of
pleasure to help create my soul
and bliss.
—Bliss
never passes.
Flowers split the ice—blue, black &
rose they rise to honor us. No, not
honor us.
To make the same melody and cry
as I and all creatures.

THERE IS NO MATTER THAT MAY BE WEIGHED AND
COUNTED!

Not ounce nor gram is heavier than
newborn love and bodies!

COCK DISAPPEARS WITHIN THY LOVE.
Unpreciseness tortures me, but inside of thee
I outward flow, and measure becomes a horror.
Thy moist warmth and rustling eyes
remind me that there is no size
except before my hands and fingertips
that meet beneath thy back.

OH WHEEL OF LOVE THAT ROLLS UPON THE PILLOWS!!!
Haired mount, and nipples
smooth and creased.

LOVE-my-Soul! Flesh cave for my protection.


LOVE-SOUL! FLESH CAVE FOR MY PROTECTION!


Thou we!


THOORAH!

Each word or act or deed or hate or petty jealousy—A PLUNGE!
A paw print unrepeatable and unsubtractable!

---

OH NO. OH NO THOU !

---

HOHH THAHHR ! !

---

NOT YET !

Not yet do we return to where we've never been.

Do waves dot-form black faces there
and we remember SELVES?
Beast profiles of pre-primordial substance, singing
immortal melodies of forgotten
questions, rise and smile at one another!

A PLACE BEFORE AND AFTER FREE MEN
ABSORBED SOCIETY !

Thy eyes and thighs and girl's snarl
of sexual bliss set free!

A groaning tear made whole with shout!!

A kiss!

YES, DAMN THE LAWS AND DAMN THE RULES
AND SYSTEMS,
EVEN DAMN THE MUSIC
through the floor!! Reach out and smile in striving!

BE HERE SOUL AND SPIRIT ! ! !

Soul is an invention.

Bodies warmth on warmth created one beginning
and repeating they break down the armor
of the universe. We join and fly and bless
unique and higher. Knowing purer
truer things! BUT HOW

did I arrive here

hand on soft hand and smile on smile?

WHERE WERE YOU IN MY BEGINNING UNLESS
WE'RE SINGING LATER?

Smile in hand.

(Living dream on far flesh.)

LIVING BATH OF EVER, FOR TRANSCENDENT
STAR OF FLESH ! ! !
I don't believe it though the mind-snake
furls itself into the night!
I am not your *plight* nor you my *ever!*

THERE ARE NOT FIELDS THAT COUNTERACT EACH
OTHER

nor Relativities!
Truth is not immortal but its shape is,
and though it changes with the Body-spirit
it is not a relativity.
There is you and I and each other
AND THIS FLOWER
of energy and bliss and pleasure
and nurtured hate
(becoming something else) we lay
upon another's body
pretending that we know all things from our void
and then forgetting it. We SPRAY becoming plumes
of beauty; we swirl with grace into a blueblack
mist with thoughts returning in the images
that no mad or sane
person will deny.

NOT THOUGHT !

NO NOT THOUGHT !
but pictures made into a cry
of future physics.

THE BUTTERFLY IS FRUITING BODY OF THE PLASM
SENT FORTH—
but the equal lion is permanent
A MAMMAL! Beating on his love,
a soul to accompany his spirit.
With hot blood the body is the spirit.
But Bacterium is sheer
technician of his eternity
—and all here now immortalities!
LIFE IS NOT THOUGHT, NOT INTELLECT, BUT
PERFECT CREATION—and another thing
there is no word for—nor
ever will be but in lovely
R A V I N G !
What is that other thing?
What Drama?
What sword and blood and purring
and touch and taste and lick
and smell that burned in rounded
youth
blaaaaaaaaaaaaah!

An estate of majesty!

A PERFECT TIT.

An inspired delicacy of sense.

AN OUTBURST OF A UNIVERSE
beyond conceived of
molecules of matter, or
any other kind . . .

# MECHANICAL REPETITION OF PREDESTINED ACTS IS PAIN

We destroy the finite system!


The softness of my arms against thy wetness
—thy writhing rubbings against solidity
that gives and challenges
with unsure presence seeking bliss
in flow of energy within the lattice
OF OUR CELLS.

"OH! AHHH! THEE!", in smiling silence!

Cries of Love becoming soul,
or searching soul or spirit,
already lighting the future quiet
—when there are flesh wavelets
of enlightened particles of self
called cells awakening
the purity of a new born
and flowing system . . .

EYES AND TONGUES KISSING.


Striped coverlets in air!

The finality of quiet is torn like paper.

# IF CONSCIOUSNESS OF LIGHT IS LIGHT
## CAN FLESH PASS OVER?

NO!
It cannot!
May intellect have speed and become the universe like
light does? Will it then create itself and shower
meat upon our bones and give us space to swing in?
You are not closed in such a trap!
Such thought is metaphor—
a happy prolog to the drama of revival that is con-
tinuation . . . Light or intellect (or soul)
is no perfection.

Meat on flesh is not a mechanism.

Pillows sprayed with flowers of silk
put there by hand
and soul's love
of decoration.

Helix-corridors of mental plight
rejuvenated by new solidity
and not the shit of matter!

HAIL THEE
3 D reality made manifest—
thy self's message
to me.
Revolutionary clouds fiery within us.

AND WHAT PEACE OF JOYOUS SWEETNESS
in the farther away than night . . .
echoing NOTHING NOTHING NOTHING more than
what I send there. Thy makings
here. Where
thou art plumed blossom
of smoothest flesh beneath me in
now and then and future time that we deny

and touch with faintest white tip
of finger. That kiss
on shoulder takes wing and flies
to there announcing our proceeding
when we blend our flesh in . . .
AHH NO AND YES!
The surface of the teeth is an illusion
for they are grottos lovely
and infinite as a perfect toe
that presses to my back or neck
in love. And pressure too
is an illusion when thou
sing in sheer flesh.


We know it.

They know it.

Listen.

NOR IS THERE THEY—BUT THOU ONLY—AND I.
We are *thy and my* perfect ones.

HERE WE FLAIL AND STAMP OURSELVES IN
GENTLENESS.
Wavebeats are clear imagination
made into thee and I from
selves of futurity
from a pool that never is.
AND THAT IS HAPPINESS!
The Night beckons and we close
our ears and eyes. Praise!
The twirl of pleasure fills
what is here. The arms and calves
spasm and shake themselves at
unmade destinies!
Separate thoughts leap into the dark
to create a universe we do
not need nor care to summon.
Sure of what is here
and happening
we sing a melody

of cloudy flesh we kiss

and dream believing

lick and love.

SURENESS OF EYES THAT FLASH ANYWAY!

The beings that we prefigure
are not loftier
than we
but are ourselves bathed
in drunken one-ness
indescribable.
Denying soul in spirit's honor
is a gesture.
Denying Deity


makes clear the *fire!*


Thy breasts and hair
and skin velvet thighs
are clearer
to the consciousness
I find.
I see all things from
an edge
in unimpassioned contemplation
and yet that consciousness
melts down the universe
like mercury or water
and it flows to and from
me making love that sprang
from Thee to me—
and passes I to Thou
and it becomes
the flesh we recognize!

Wine is that which fills
the night beyond
the farthest touch
—is sugar made into
a nebular ocean
beyond the barrier
of photons

that
hypnotize our eyes.
We touch upon that place
packed so tight with bliss
there is not
even room for light
to fly there.
Consciousness assumes
that passion
is flesh
and separates itself to gain
a knowledge—knowing
that if flesh is passion
the intellect is trick.
And it raises high
the device as instrument,
meat instrument, of imagination.
—Its purpose is to touch
the night.
The unimpassioned gives
way in exuberance and admits
that it is highest
when it touches thee
and has its meaning.
THE DRAMA IS PERFORMED,
AND SCENE AND ACT
MAKE EVIDENT
shortcomings of
the highest View,
for a rose-shaped nipple
may be immortal more
than we ever knew or dared
admit. When universe melts
into a silver flow
and the pictures
in the mind grow many-colored,
the view or consciousness
gives way!
I love Thee and thou art
solid touch upon my ghost-
liness, that I believe

and name time after time
with name of view or
vision—BUT THOU ART THERE!
Affirmative not by
mental state, or only
beauteous word, but
in soft arm manifest
and moistened lip
and beating heart
and padded bone
and hair and tissue.
When I believe myself with
thee, or after thy departing,
I am more inspired
by what I do not know!
We have melted down with
love
a barricade.
I count out my loves upon thy
imaginary back when you have
left me. And my spirit
becoming soul, I once
again acknowledge,
spans into the night or
noon or morn—
and comes back with
a new flower—pure and untorn.

# DRUNK VARIATION

I WILL NOT GIVE YOU BEAUTY! There
is but one beauty. Without proportion

within my skull. In
my eyes!

BUT OH! OH! What is that I see
in your gray eyes? There are skies!
Skies of new grace and action!
You are the one I have worshipped
while you honored me.
Together we shall wear new costumes.
(New hair, eyes, breasts, and breath
—new pads of tenderness.)
We shall flee
this grim scene
on winged feet.
Acknowledge that we are meat
fated to unending praise!

---

FLECK BOOT MERCURY GOBLET

# GRAHR MANTRA

### 1.

Blue Black Winged Space Rainbow GRAHHR
GRAHHR GRAHHR GRAHHR Blue
Black Winged GRAHHR Rainbow
Rainbow Space Rainbow Black
Hahr Yahr Pink Thunder Vapor
GRAH!   GRAH!
Black leather
and sweet toes.

### 2.

Blue Black Winged Space Rainbow GRAHHR
Toes Kiss White Rainbow Mount
GRAHHR Leather Winged Black GRAHHR
Space Pink GRAH Vapor
Thunder Leather White GRAHHR Toes
GRAH!   GRAH!
Black Rainbow
Space toes.

### 3.

Blue Black Winged Space Rainbow GRAHHR
Black Winged GRAHHR Toes Kiss
Pink Leather GRAHHR Blue Rainbow
Vapor GRAHHR Vapor GRAHHR
Hahr Rainbow Space Black Yahr
GRAH!   GRAH!
White Mount Toes Kiss
Toes Kiss Star.

# POISONED
# WHEAT

------------------

# OH, BLUE GRAY GREEN PALE GRAHHR!
## TRANQUIL POURING ROSE LION SALT!

There is death in Viet Nam!
There is death in Viet Nam!
There is death in Viet Nam!
And our bodies are mad with the forgotten
memory that we are creatures!

*Blue-black skull rose lust boot!*

Citizens of the United States
are in the hands of traitors
who ignore their will and force
them into silent acceptance
of needless and undesired warfare.

EACH MAN, WOMAN, CHILD
*is innocent*
and not responsible
for the atrocities committed by any
government. Mistakes, hypocrisies, crimes
that result in the present
FASCISM
are made in the past in
HISTORY.
Structural mechanisms of Society
create guilt in the individual.
((Now it is worst when man is at the edge,
he may be freed of his
carnivore past—and is on the verge
of becoming a singer and glorious creature
borne free through the universe.
Soon no lamb or man
may be eaten
save

with the smile of sacrifice!))

It is our nature to explore
that which is called Evil
by the haters of matter
and pleasure. But GUILT
is untenable! Guilt is not
inheritable. Acceptance of guilt
for a Capitalist heritage creates fear.

NO ONE IS CULPABLE FOR THESE CRIMES!
We are flowers capable of creating the seeds
and fruit of new liberty.
Like beautiful flowers the profits of Capitalist
society are the blossoming
of the agonized labor and starvation
of the world's masses.
THAT I AM A FLOWER DOES NOT MEAN
THAT I AM RESPONSIBLE
FOR THE AGONY OF THE ROOTS!
But, as a man, I am conscious of the agony,
labor, pain. And murders take place
for Society!

Acceptance of guilt for the acts of
entrepreneurs, capitalists and imperialists
smothers, tricks, and stupefies

the free creature! He will, is, driven
to fear, racism, and inaction!

If I forget, for a prolonged moment,
the mammal, sensory pleasure of which
I am capable
I must toil to override
the creeping guilt that destroys
me spiritually!

I AM NOT GUILTY!

I AM A LIVING CREATURE!

# I AM NOT RESPONSIBLE FOR THE TRAITOROUS FASCISM AND TOTALITARIANISM THAT SURROUND me!!!

((The definitions of *fascism* and *totalitarianism*
must be reviewed in light of the new media developed
by technology. The nature of the human
mammal is being remade and it is time for
redefinitions . . . ))

I AM NOT RESPONSIBLE
FOR THOSE WHO HAVE CREATED
AND / OR CAPTURED the CONTROL DEVICES
OF THE SOCIETY THAT SURROUNDS ME!
I despise Society that creates
bundles of individual cruelties
and presses them en masse
against the helpless.

I AM INNOCENT! In my innocence I may act creatively
and *not* fulfill a pre-prescribed pattern
of guilt leading to escapism and cynicism.

COMMUNISM WILL NOT WORK!
Communism will not create food in quantities
necessary for man's survival.

CAPITALISM IS FAILURE!
It creates overpopulation, slavery,
and starvation.

Whether I be in Soviet Russia, Red China, or Imperialist
England or France, or Capitalist United States,
I am not responsible for the fascist
or totalitarian crimes
that are whitewashed
under the name *Modern History!*
I AM INNOCENT AND FREE!
I AM A MAMMAL!
I AM A WARM-BLOODED SENSORY CREATURE

CAPABLE OF LOVE AND HATE AND ACTION AND
INACTION!
CAPABLE OF GUILT AND CAPABLE
OF SPEECH AND STRIVING!

—I am sickened by the thought
(and photographs)
of cruel and vicious executions
and tortures of Asian
and Algerian soldiers.

I AM SICKENED
by the oncoming MASS STARVATION
and the concomitant revolting degree
of overpopulation, and the accompanying
production of incredible numbers
of useless physical objects
whose raw materials demand
a destruction of those parts of nature
I have come to think of as beautiful!
—THOUGH I REJOICE IN THE FOREST
AND CAVES OF THE FUTURE!

BEING SICKENED IS A LUXURY
that I cannot afford without loss
of spirit, gradually
becoming irreparable! I am a man!
Sickness *and* guilt must be cast off!
Guilt is a luxury.
Being sickened is meaningless.
CAPITALISM AND COMMUNISM ARE A POLITICAL
CONFRONTATION!

I have escaped politics. I disavow
the meeting whether it is a means to
war or coexistence!
The meanings of Marxism and Laissez-faire
are extinct.
The population of the United States will double
by the year 2000. Certain South American
nations double each eighteen and twenty years.

There is no answer
but a multiplicity of answers created by men.
A large proportion of men are on the verge
OF STARVATION!
When density of creature to creature reaches
a certain degree
the ultra-crowded condition is a
biological sink.
Rats in overpopulation experiments
become insane in predictable types . . .
perverts, cannibals, hoods, criminals, and semi-
catatonics. When crowding reaches a certain
point the animals respond by more need
and desire
for crowding!
!SAN FRANCISCO, TOKYO, LONDON, MOSCOW, PEKING!

The human being is the commonest object!

Each human being must be responded to.
There are too many for the nervous system.
Man evolved as a social creature
and rare animal. He is now
the commonest large animal
—and threatens all other creatures with extinction.


((In the Neolithic, men made both plants and animals
subject to his appetites through cultivation
and domestication—the stress
of this guilt began a genetic change in his
being. He mutated himself—population
began.
Now he is capable of freeing himself
from the Neolithic Revolution
and must choose between
song and suicide!))


Cynicism and escapism are the shapes
of reaction to the torture and slaughter

of Asians, Asians placed
in overpopulation and starvation
by European and American imperialism . . .
By outright conquest and introduction
of technology into non-technological nations.
Colonial nations are directed to produce
products desired by the West.
They are trained as consumers
of Western material artifacts.
They are given Western medicine which lowers
the mortality rate.

If an American accepts these facts he must assume
guilt and responsibility!
THIS IS NOT SO! Society will have
the individual feel guilt so that he will fly
from the possibility of action.
SOCIETY WILL THEN PERPETUATE THE STATUS QUO OF
SOCIETY!
But this is not true for Society is insane.
A status quo is not being perpetuated.
Society is masochistic.
It deludes itself that a status quo is
maintained. It is driving for its destruction.
WESTERN SOCIETY HAS ALREADY DESTROYED ITSELF!
The Culture is extinct! The last sentry
at the gate has pressed the muzzle to his
forehead and pulled the trigger!
The new civilization will not be communism!
POLITICS ARE AS DEAD AS THE CULTURE
they supported!
Politics are theories regarding the speculated
laws of power—their applications
have never touched men except in shapes
of repression!
NEW SOCIETY WILL BE BIOLOGICAL!

HISTORY IS INVALID BECAUSE WE ARE ESCAPED
FROM HISTORY. As individuals we inhabit
a plateau where civilization is perpetuated
by the mechanisms of a rapidly dying and masochistic

Society. We are supported by traitors
and barbarians who operate war
utilizing the business principles of this Society.


THOSE WHO CAN SEE AND FEEL ARE IN HIDING THEY
HOPE
for a few years of life before the holocaust.
They are caught up in the forms of evangelism
that are hysterical reaction
to population density. They hope
for a miracle. The thrill of the beauty
of the new music and entertainment media—as well
as religion—are evangelism.
It is beautiful that even hysteria can be made
to give assurance and pleasure and some means
of satisfaction
—BUT IT IS A LAST DITCH BIOLOGICAL REACTION

The small hope for salvation by means of utilization
of hysteria is pathetic!!!!!

The bombing of Asian fishing villages can be equated
to the new music / / save that one is beautiful
and one is not. The witness of the new intellectuals
testifies to the beauty of both!

Beauty IS hideous!
Mussolini spoke of the beauty of bombing
villages as the SS cherished the pleasure
of executing Jews! ((What INSANITY
to have Israel as thorn to the Arabs!))

The human mammal is not capable of receiving pleasure
from the tortured deaths of his own kind
without previous acceptance of insanity
or the development of insanity
within himself!
The masses of planes that fly over

ARE NOT PASSENGER SHIPS

but are bombers flying to Asia!

STOP UP THE EARS—it is true!

AND WHO IS FLYING THEM?

What name for those who accept authority
and enter the cockpits?
No doubt as in the bombing of Guernica!

What name for the voice of authority that tells
the pilots to enter the ships?

THE ACCEPTANCE OF THE IMPOSSIBLE IS CYNICISM!
To admire or be silent about pain and death
IS CYNICISM!
To enact a role when Society is a corpse
IS CYNICISM!

Whether the corpse be a young Soviet or Chinese or an old
U.S. corpse!

WITHDRAWAL FROM INFORMATION IS ESCAPISM!
*Escape from the ears that hear the bombers pass?*
Evangelism—whether it be of art or religion
is escapism.
There must be a milieu for action.
Barbarism,
Atrocities,
Bombings,
Poisonings
of wheat in Cambodia,
Secret Government agencies,

and all manifestations of political hysteria

LEAD TO GENOCIDE! OR MASS STARVATION
and such Hell that death would be better!

FREEDOM FROM GUILT AND RESPONSIBILITY
is necessary to the individual so he may

receive the normal pleasures of body and life
—whether it be the pleasures of a Congo tribesman
or a city dweller in a European or American city!

IDEALISM IS EASY FOR THE MOST WEALTHY AND THE
MOST IMPOVERISHED!

POLITICS IS DEAD AND BIOLOGY IS HERE!

FEAR AND GUILT MUST BE CAST ASIDE LIKE A DIRTY
ROBE!

CYNICISM AND ESCAPISM MUST BE PUT ASIDE
INSTANTLY!

The traitors directing the barbarism must have power taken
from them!

There is no single answer to the new biological confrontation!
There must be a multitude of solutions!
They must be arrived at by thought and action.
Neither is possible without energy and information!

Society and Government smother both energy and information!

The majority of the citizens are against the war!
War creates guilt that causes blindness!

Blindness means hysteria and flight!

An arena must be cleared for new thought and action
that is not national in scope
but incorporates all human creatures . . .
and all creatures to come!
—All who will move to the stars to investigate
the possibilities of infinite freedoms.

EACH MAN IS INNOCENT!
The point of life is not rest but action.
DEATH IS REST
—everyone will have enough rest for eternity!

NOW IS THE TIME FOR ACTION.
THE WAR MUST BE STOPPED—THE WORLD SEEN
CLEARLY!

THE UNIVERSE IS MESSIAH!

WHAT IS THIS SMOKE?

The neon napalm flash is filth and death!

GRAHH!          BLESS!

# FOR KENNETH ANGER

THE NEW MAN SHALL BE AS BEAUTIFUL AS THE WOMAN
AS PROUD, AS FREE AND NAKED
of all horror—of all shame
AND ALCHEMICAL
in Ferocity and Gentleness.
Right hand shall bless the left.
Torturer and Executioner—as beloved as the death
of the victim! Liberty shall be
what the white finger touches
and black shall be the finger touching it.
!OH GRAHR!
Bleshk grahhr nah murder droon breeth dappled mint.

WHAN THAH GROOOHR EEN DREEM
WHAH SHALAHN—OH—EEM BLEZZ
ehn el rainbow whar hroosh voice. Brah! Gragreer!
OH! OH! OH! OOOH! Black bombers hissing and spurting.
Mountains.
Trees. Cactus. Violet Clouds. Cool rivers. Breast Dream can
Violence.
Children pelted with flowers on a cliff
in the Sunset!

THE NEW MAN SHALL BE AS BEAUTIFUL AS THE
WOMAN!
AS PROUD, AS FREE AND NAKED
of all horror—of all shame
AND ALCHEMICAL
in Ferocity and Gentleness.
New man springs from murder and kindness!
Woman lies by his side making a song
to comfort him.
Eyes are bright on the new Film.

Each man a creep—a rotten failure
creating new arms

# TO BUILD A HEAVEN

with hair to his ass and strange clothes
rejecting the guilt and shame!

RESPONSIBILITY IS AS DEAD AS ITS EARLIEST VICTIM!

The Parasites are not sorry
and make amends! The Filth—the C.I.A.,
the Generals, the Air Force, and Rand Corp,
THE STARVERS—The Wooden and Hostile,
THE DECADENT, DISTORTERS OF BABES,
Liberals and Conservatives
(Forgetting they are mammals served
by machines!)
brought to their knees before the youth
of any man or woman
cry out with a strange voice!

Slaves murder children and the Soft
are nauseous as they writhe-dance
in the streets brought together
by biological love. The Da Vincian
voice of gene and hormone! NEW MAN

CREATES HIMSELF IN THE CAVE LIGHTED BY HIS
SENSES!
Each man is a mess and a fuck-up
with hideous ideals
serving his perverted individual
HOLY GHOST
with a twisted smile!

BUT HOW BEAUTIFUL! HOW BEAUTIFUL!

—And what grace!

# OVERPOP

THIS IS SHEER JOY *TRES MUCHO* TO BE ALIVE
WHEN THE UNIVERSE IS MESSIAH!
NOW IS MY RED ROAR CAR! NOW IS MY MUSCLE ARM!

Joy that I shall be dead to rest for ten billion
tomorrows! Sweet the rose,
and presto the plum blossom!
Hail to the sharp spikes and dry pillows!
Bless the satins and the musical
voices! Love to the huge faces
that smile upon me!
Bless the green money that vanishes
in the pockets of the corruptors!
NOW I AM ALIVE!
Gold Leather Sneer Plump Petal!
Black smoke of white petals!
Multitudinous energies and food for the lucky!
*AHG!!!!!*
This is agony!

# VARIATION

!MORTALITY IS BEAUTY THE BEAST SPIRIT LIVES
FOREVER!

—AND THE SOUL SINGS
laughing in the moving thigh!
The stars are nuclei
within the speeding cell!
Passing faces trap the bounds
of joy! Boots sound taps
upon eternity! Capes rustle
on the gates of Hell!

The soft blue rose—immortal as I!

Your high-heeled image lives!

Your gracious lips!

Fire is not made to die!

# MANTRA

JESUS, I AM SICK OF THE SPIRITUAL WARFARE!!!!
YES, HERE WE ARE IN THE DEATH OF HELL!
O.K., black rose thunder!
O.K., black rose thunder!
O.K., black rose thunder!
Your bodies and kisses are my
ETERNITY!

Fleck Boot Mercury Vapor!

# WILLIAM H. BONNEY: BILLY THE KID

BLACK STAR VIOLET BRONZE BLUE PAIN, I SEE YOUR
FACE
SLASHED BY X'S. I know thy stain!
For spirit meat contains the fewest strictures.

The sufferings of your body are the outlines
of energy that take the shape
of unfelt desire!
PAINS ARE MOVIES


of unfilled loves!

---

My pains are never real
but only joys in flight
that smash against
a muscle wall and drop
like hummingbirds
to pant and die
beneath a plate of glass

or crush their breasts on an adobe wall!

# CUPID'S GRIN

*for Sterling Bunnell*

YES! THIS DAMN UNIVERSE!
An ever-flowing, eternal, closed up,
open system—a dial of vibratory flows
from end to front—a technicolor timeless object—
STARS—STARS—NEBULAE—AND SWIRLS
of growing energy that fantasizes self.
A LIVING STATUE OF A SONG!
(Amoeba daydreams Metazoa.
Helium imagines Milky Way!
Or start from either end.)
ALIVE AS THE SEA!
When it all begins
I'll be there.
You'll know me by my curling lips

—AND CHUCKLE
!

# MATTER

MATTER IS ALIVE, BY GOD!
MATTER IS ALIVE!
The grains of crystal slide.
It is the molecular consciousness!
(((I must be a Pagan
to survive it
—TO SURVIVE
this vision.
With grinning teeth!))
It takes its shape.
Fanatic Will.
Dripping. Pouring. Pressing.
HAH!

# THE SERMONS OF JEAN HARLOW
## & 
## THE CURSES OF BILLY THE KID

## HARLOW:


*OH GOD, HOW SUPERB IT IS, TO BE INFINITELY*
*BEAUTIFUL!*
*OH GOD, AMONG THE PLUMES AND RAINBOWS*
*floating in air! I LOVE IT!*
*And the dark woods!—My arms among them!*
*THE GLIMMER OF THE PLANKS OF THE VEIL*
*making all this! Do you see it!? It is sheer,*
*REALLY ALL SHEER!*
*Oh, thank God, I am breathing*
*and I lift my chin in the air!*
*I feel my breasts move*
*and the muscles in them*
*make circles*
*and the blood warms the back of my neck*
*and my slender arms bulge!*
*My blonde hair falls in my face*
*and my mouth breathes in*
*almost making a smile . . .*
*And I reach one finger*
*into the air*
*and press it—it giggles at me*
*my surprise to see*
*and I fall*
*in the hall*
*of my senses. Touching the hole*
*to love. AHH! OH! OH!*
*OOOOOOOHHHHHHH*

# THE KID:


THANK GOD I AM HERE! I WILL KILL ALL THOSE
WHO OFFEND ME
THEN I'LL STEP THROUGH THE RAINBOW
at the top of the Cliff! I'll walk
on them, with my plumed boots in their faces,
I shall run over their chests
and dance naked on their children
with the moon behind me making a sil-
houette! GOD DAMN THESE FUCKING BASTARDS
WHO KILL!!
I'll destroy each
of them! AND THEN I'LL TORTURE
THEIR SOULS
in Hell!!!!
TANK
KNIFE
CRASHER!!
Rose
WAVE
drip
breath
sweet
INFERNO!

# HARLOW:

*OH GOD I WANT TO TELL YOU I LOVE YOU,*
*WITH OR WITHOUT THE PAINT ON MY LIPS.*
*Oh God, I love you as the slips*
*of flowers blossoming in May*
*or the chrome sportscar*
*exploding in play!*
*IT IS ALL REAL—I THINK,*
*as an ankle in satin*
*of blue or of cream*
*in the dream-stream where thoughts beam!*
*And I step from the wreck with a grin*
*one speck of oil on my shin*
*and roll my eyes upward*
*to*
*YOU . . .*
*Not even the strap on my slip*
*is broken.*

*And the sky is turquoise melting into blue!*
*AND THE SKY IS TURQUOISE MELTING INTO BLUE.*

# THE KID:


IT IS ALL A GRAY HELL! THE BLUES BECOME GRAY!
Only a dark brown or a black is worth seeing.
The elves and the fairies are flayed!
Man and God are to blame
for the cruelty and thieving
seething in the kettle!
I've torn the wings off my skull,
but I'll raise
myself in the blaze
by my eyeballs. With my
arms crossed behind my back
grasping my toes in the flack
of the bombs exploding,
while the splashed flames daze
themselves on human meat!
I
SHALL RAISE
MYSELF WITH MY FACE
A YELLOW MASK OF FURY!!!!

## HARLOW:

THE SKY IS TURQUOISE MELTING TO BLUE,
the sky is turquoise melting to blue,
and I love you true
OH GOD!
Oh God in my shape
sweet as a grape
covered with silk and with lace.
I see your white face
loaded with grace
floating in my oval mirror.
The ivory handle loves my hand
the scent of flowers fills the room
where I stand,
while I float ten feet in the air.
Oh, I am true, true, true,
to me and to you and to the fantasy
of my calves. The sunlight burns my skin
but I grow plump in your grace
sailing in the space
where you make me of my dream.
OH.
AHHH
OOOOOOOOOH,
a rhinestone kiss for you . . .
A beaded bag . . .
A satin slipper . . .
And I shall be true to a thousand loves
like mascara melting on skin.

# THE KID:

WE COIL OUR SKINS IN SMOKE—AS TWISTED AS A
FILTHY JOKE.
One lost in the other, turned inside out
upon a spit we make
for each other!
And I stand free
with utter contempt I pee
upon my heap of gold
like a Cherub in a Dionysian Park.
YEAH, it is dark,
owls and bats play with the salamandrine
shark, rotting in their fetish slime
and steal shit from one another.
My brain is a floating feather
in a blast of sun.
I can see ten billion years to anywhere
AND ITS ALL A SHAME!
I'll take one crime and compound it
to a hero's deed
upon a blueblack bridge
OF ICE
and cool my shotgun with a slice
of sheriff's life! HO HUMM!
That's not real!
THAT'S NOT REAL! There's a coil
of sable wire with thorns
that blows this shit to Hell!
And pictures change shape upon a sandy floor!
Oh Yeah!
*Crack!*

## HARLOW:

*Turn on and sing my happy song,*
*Oh God,*
*and I'll be you!*
*The way is not long*
*and I am strong*
*as an Easter April wrapped in red,*
*the skies are alive or dead,*
*no difference when you are there, if you are—*
*IT DOES NOT MATTER*
*I dance in your glance with toes like fur*
*I furl myself in air with platinum hair*
*that drifts in the glare of You*
*becoming Me. And I see*
*my dress drop to the floor*
*upon the beaming knitted rug.*
*I thank me for my arms and thank you*
*for your charms, and me*
*for my lacquered nails with moons*
*that wax and wane,*
*and I know that sane*
*or insane*
*DOES NOT MATTER*
*with taxi driver*
*or with Duke. Turn on*
*and sing my happy song*
*AND I'LL BE YOU . . .*

## THE KID:

LIKE NEW OLD JAZZ COMING THROUGH THE WALLS!
The sound of sickening piano
where owl-eyed feathers
TURN TO FLAME
and burn like heather
on an earth turned Gates of Hell destroyed by shame!
The pleasure mongers feel
themselves and peel
their grape.
THE SHIT OF DEATH'S AN ORANGE WALL
that changes shape and crackles!!
DISEMBODIED VOICES FLOAT IN AIR!
and
I DON'T CARE A HAIR.
The cougar and the spider float in their garbage boat
upon the waves of lead.
GOD DAMN YOU! DIE! BE DEAD!
With a buckshot blast
accompanying the last words of Man!
The human tiger wears a lambkin's skin
AND SCREAMS
his dreams
into
a hair-lined
PIT!
I'll make it *new!*

# *HARLOW* & THE KID:

*Rise up! Rise up! The voicelet cries,*
*the days are a bracelet in your eyes*
*of filigree and silvered gold*
*the nights shall never paralyze*

•

The Pain that withers in the fold
and bags of flesh and skin that shies
where Babe-in-Youth once laughed and rolled
beneath a light of leather skies

•

*The softness of my flesh that swings*
*before a mild curtain of strings*
*of colored glass that blows and gleams*
*like varnished wood beheld by wings*

•

And faces drip upon the beams
like torturesques of sagging meat
and silhouettes in crushing streams
break up, and tug and pull the sheet

Where men are halves, dust does not float
OH DRUNKEN
*Drunken*
DRUNKEN
*Drunken*
DRUNKEN
*Drunken*
DRUNKEN
*Drunken*
DRUNKEN
*Drunken*

HELL OF JOY where we swirl
and furl
THE CYCLONES OF LOVERS
*in a dream, in a swarm, where it's warm,*
*above the soft and polished machines like bees*
*becoming angels sipping on a neon pelt.*
Like a hideous charm exploded
to the size of a world
but touching cheeks again
and human above the wooden flames!
BUT HERE IS MY HAND—I AM REAL AGAIN.
*Here is my breast I am real again,*
*the nipple is a rose . . .*

HERE IS MY THORN, MY HATE IS A BUD . . .

*Here is my smile that floats leaving a trail*
*of laughs . . .*
*HERE ARE MY WINGS THAT BEAT . . .*
*In ice & in heat?*
YEAH!
YES!
*The Universe creating a face*
*peeping from a cushioned cave*
*in fleeting guises of meat . . .*
ETERNALLY . . .        FOREVER . . .

# VIET NAM SONG

Platinum fur and brass revolver shine
Love Lion, Lioness are dead
And the U.S. ground is red
And everything is going fine
With platinum fur and brass revolver shine
—with sweet dust of gun and white neck

It's time, it's time, I know it's time
To tell that Love Lion, Lioness
are alive!
With platinum fur and brass revolver shine
—with sweet dust of gun and white neck

People say, "Don't get out of line
Love Lion, Lioness are dead"
And the U.S. ground is red
with Oriental blood
Platinum fur and brass revolver shine
—with sweet dust of gun and white neck

With lace and fur and sugared blood
With fur and leather whirr and creak
Till they learn how to speak
—Love Lion, Lioness
are alive!
—with sweet dust of gun and white neck

# LIBERATION
*for Freewheelin Frank*


I DEDICATE MYSELF TO BE SENT A MULTITUDE OF NEW
WAYS!
THE HARP SHALL BE MY WAY!
I SHALL BE A CRIMINAL AND AN HONEST MAN
NEON AND MEAT
IN THE CHROME DEAD STREET
FINDING NEW LOVE LIKE WINE
WHILE THE HARPIES CAW
AND PREACH THEMSELVES
TO ME
I sing the curse of beauty.

# After
# Thoughts

1. The poems in *The New Book / A Book of Torture* were written spontaneously and were the only regimen that I could maintain at the time.

2. It was 1959 and I was twenty-seven. Writing these poems, I imagined it as one long poem. That was as coherent as I could be. Sometimes while writing I imagined I was Shelley, sometimes I imagined I was Antonin Artaud.

3. Sometimes I was my grieved, weak, and shaking self, in the midst of a dark night of the soul, sexual adventures and idealisms, and psychedelics.

4. Sometimes I was a god like Goethe, or like pianist Bud Powell playing "Autumn in New York."

5. I was looking for inspiration and wanted to see my muscles and the physique of my breath in lines and stanzas of poetry. A goal was to make a gestural poetry like the painting of Pollock, Kline, and Clyfford Still.

6. Later, "Love Lion Book," a long poem in *Star*, was written and rewritten, like a string quartet, over four years' time. I wanted to make an erotic, mystical, philosophical poem not unlike certain old Arabic poems.

7. For "Love Lion Book" I ransacked dictionaries and lexicons for words like "ambassage" and mixed them with *grahhhr*s and sounds in

the Beast Language that I had invented earlier (in my book *Ghost Tantras*).

8. At one pole of writing I was making poetry from the stark, enigmatic reality of a peyote depression, and at the other pole I wrote a spontaneous homage to Wolf Robe in the midst of a seemingly unrelated poem.

9. During the Fifties, a community of artists vigorously supported and energetically competed with one another in San Francisco. The young poets' criticisms of each other forced new subject matter into being.

10. We fiercely and happily created new territory for ourselves and each other.

11. The sound made by new territory spills from real life into the media and politics; after the postwar silence our voices seemed very loud.

12. We were outlaws—still today, people of deep or myriad feeling are outlaws. I hated the state that sent formations of supply planes over my San Francisco house to unload napalm, frozen meat, and herbicides in Vietnam. "Poisoned Wheat," which is collected in *Star*, was the first long poem condemning the U.S. massacre in Southeast Asia.

13. Billy the Kid and Jean Harlow became obsessed with me and stood by my desk and performed a play as I wrote it down. When *The Beard* was performed it was arrested in San Francisco, Berkeley, Los Angeles, and Vancouver, while it won prizes in New York and praises in London and Paris.

14. Billy the Kid and Jean Harlow would not go away after the scandal over the play, *The Beard*, died down. They stood at my bed late at night till I wrote down *"The Sermons of Jean Harlow* & the Curses of Billy the Kid." This set of songs is collected in *Star* shortly following "Poisoned Wheat."

15. When one gently shakes *Huge Dreams*, the sounds of the Beatles and the Stones can be heard, but it's the sound of the times, before corporations, beer, hi-fi equipment, and cologne bought up music.

16. In *Huge Dreams*, Leadbelly, Monteverdi's operas, Thelonious Monk, and Miles Davis can be heard along with the voice of Anita O'Day and the breath of Emily Dickinson.

17. *"The Sermons of Jean Harlow* & the Curses of Billy the Kid" and "Love Lion Book" and "13 Mad Sonnets" were published as small books by fine printers and small press publishers who ranged from renegade book dealers to Italian designer Ettore Sottsass.

18. *The New Book / A Book of Torture* made a space for my young manhood to see and move through. The dark night ends in *Star* in "Mad Sonnet 6" and "Mad Sonnet 7." In *Star* the poetry becomes clearer. The two books are layers of one consciousness.

19. I submitted "The Surge" to *Scientific American*—when it was rejected, Frontier Press published it as a small avant-garde book. I was being taught by my biologist friends on field trips that ranged from Death Valley to Kenya. One friend loaned me his library of nature and biology, which we took to my apartment in the Haight with a window looking on the ocean.

20. Some poets experimented with mantras and sound texts and I used beast-language sounds and phrases for tantric purposes, to change the nature of reality. The beast language got into songs I wrote with my autoharp and also into poems in *Star*.

21. When the flower people moved into the Haight, the Beats became their advisers. But we learned from them—as we had from San Francisco anarchist circles and the Eastern philosophies of the Pacific rim.

22. In the Fifties psychedelic drugs opened portholes to reality and were taken with respect, but there was also delusion and collusion. It was powerful alchemy and we were poets, yogins, scientists, and

philosophers inhabiting a post–World War II world that was cata-
tonic and cold with materialism, lovelessness, and conformity.

23. Writing *The New Book / A Book of Torture* was an act made
to free myself, and, hopefully, to help anyone who could use the po-
ems. I was also struggling with essays and my first plays. I shifted
ground while writing "13 Mad Sonnets"; I wanted to re-invent
beauty, which I had rejected. I wanted to begin soul-making in a
larger world. I wrote my first novel, *The Mad Cub*, in 1964, to make
sure that I would not lose my memory of childhood and young man-
hood.

24. It was not possible for me to move ahead without writing poems
like "Rant Block" and "The Column," which are in *The New Book /
A Book of Torture*. I was making poetry in which gesture, thought,
and perception are the same thing and are joined together in the im-
mediacy of writing. I was grateful for hand-made, hand-created
magazines like *Yugen* and *Semina*, where I could see my work side-
by-side with di Prima, Duncan, Burroughs, Snyder, Kerouac,
Whalen, Kyger, Olson, Creeley, and Baraka.

25. From my "Author's Note" to *Rebel Lions* in 1991:
By 1955 I began centering poems so that it would be clear that
they are the stuff of consciousness. The impulse to center the poems
(*which was unusual at the time*) gave the writing a visual notation for
the breath and voice as well as the reading mind, and it gave the po-
ems the lengthwise symmetry found in higher animals. The center-
ing also allowed the poems to have a body language on the page, and
with the voice when spoken aloud. There were other reasons too, I
could look at the integrity of the poems—as if they were creatures
and be moved by their shapes. I was not interested in what was then
called "form" but in the extension of content into a shape with an im-
mediate relation to me and to the reader.
I was interested in the poem being alive in the air as well as on the
page. The poem on the page troubled me because it seemed like
such a thing of beauty, I wanted to remind the reader that it was, in
fact, an object, and a seductive object because it was so close to be-
ing alive. By putting lines of capital letters in the text of the poem

there was a disruption of the allure of the poem and a reminder that it was a made thing. The capitals worked, on the one hand, to distance the reader for a moment and, on the other, to create an attractive disruption of an otherwise flowing experience. Later I experimented with using the lines of capitals to signify a small shift of intensity in the voice or mind. The lines of capitals at the opening of the poem came to signify the quality of energy with which a poem begins. *The capitals never mean that the lines are shouted or that they are chanted.*

My poetry . . . captures the movement of thought from perception to perception and leaves it flourishing in the normal animal energy that is our substance.

# ABOUT THE AUTHOR

Michael McClure is a poet, novelist, essayist, and playwright. His play *The Beard* provoked a censorship battle in 1968. For fourteen nights the cast was arrested after each performance.

McClure's ongoing solo poetry readings, and his performance of poetry with music, carry forward the tradition he, Allen Ginsberg, and Gary Snyder began in their first group reading at the Six Gallery in San Francisco in 1955.

According to Ray Manzarek, keyboardist for the Doors, "McClure and Jim Morrison are tapping into the same universal consciousness; that's where their poetry comes from." In recent years McClure and Manzarek have collaborated to bring their poetry and music to clubs and colleges. Their CD and video are both called *Love Lion*.

McClure has received numerous awards, including a Guggenheim Fellowship, the Obie Award for Best Play, an NEA grant, the Alfred Jarry Award, and a Rockefeller grant for playwriting. The National Poetry Association honored him for Distinguished Lifetime Achievement in Poetry.

McClure cowrote Janice Joplin's "Mercedes Benz." He recited Chaucer in Martin Scorsese's *The Last Waltz* and portrayed an outlaw motorcyclist in Norman Mailer's *Beyond the Law*. He lives with his wife, the sculptor Amy Evans McClure, in Oakland, California.

Visit Michael McClure's Web site at:
www.thing.net/~grist/lnd/mcclurec.htm

Paul Beatty
*Joker, Joker, Deuce*

Ted Berrigan
*Selected Poems*

Philip Booth
*Pairs*

Jim Carroll
*Fear of Dreaming*

Jim Carroll
*Void of Course*

Nicholas Christopher
*5° & Other Poems*

Carl Dennis
*Ranking the Wishes*

Diane di Prima
*Loba*

Stuart Dischell
*Evenings and Avenues*

Stephen Dobyns
*Common Carnage*

Paul Durcan
*A Snail in My Prime*

Amy Gerstler
*Crown of Weeds*

Amy Gerstler
*Nerve Storm*

Debora Greger
*Desert Fathers,*
*Uranium Daughters*

Robert Hunter
*Glass Lunch*

Robert Hunter
*Sentinel*

Barbara Jordan
*Trace Elements*

Jack Kerouac
*Book of Blues*

Ann Lauterbach
*And For Example*

Ann Lauterbach
*On a Stair*

William Logan
*Vain Empires*

Derek Mahon
*Selected Poems*

Michael McClure
*Huge Dreams:*
*San Francisco and Beat Poems*

Michael McClure
*Three Poems*

Carol Muske
*An Octave Above Thunder*

Alice Notley
*The Descent of Alette*

Alice Notley
*Mysteries of Small Houses*

Anne Waldman
*Kill or Cure*

Rachel Wetzsteon
*Home and Away*

Philip Whalen
*Overtime: Selected Poems*

Robert Wrigley
*In the Bank of Beautiful Sins*